THE PINNACLE:

The Contemporary American Presidency

*THE LIPPINCOTT SERIES IN
AMERICAN GOVERNMENT*

Under the editorship of William C. Havard,

Virginia Polytechnic Institute and State University

JOHN F. MURPHY
United States Coast Guard Academy

The Pinnacle:
THE CONTEMPORARY AMERICAN PRESIDENCY

J. B. LIPPINCOTT COMPANY

Philadelphia   New York   Toronto

ISBN 0–397–47312–5
Library of Congress Catalog Card Number 74–3164
Printed in the United States of America

Library of Congress Cataloging in Publication Data

Murphy, John Francis, 1922 (Aug. 20)

    The pinnacle: the contemporary American Presidency.
    (The Lippincott series in American government)
    Includes bibliographical references.
    1. United States—Politics and government—20th century. 2. Presidents—United States—Biography.
I. Title.

E743.M87	*353.03'13*	*74–3164*

ISBN 0–397–47312–5

For Rita, Sean, and Mary

CONTENTS

Introduction

World War II had three major effects on the United States: it forged the citizens into a single nation and transformed formerly local and sectional questions into national problems; it placed the federal government at the center of responsibility in every major area of American life; and it thrust the nation into the prime position in world leadership. World War II completed the American Revolution, with the induction of millions of men and women into the armed forces, by the mass migrations which it caused to take place within the national boundaries, and through the burgeoning industrialization it fostered which ignored historic sectional boundaries. This war forced the American people to create the world's most productive industrial plants at the moment Americans became history's greatest agricultural producers. The year 1945 marked the first time that it was proper to speak of "the American nation."

The end of World War II and the succession to the presidency of Harry S Truman occurred almost simultaneously. Truman was thus the first President to recognize the basic transformations made in the nation by the war and the first to bear the heavy responsibilities imposed upon the President by the changed conditions. Prior to this point, Presidents accepted their tasks with varying degrees of success, seeking emergency faculties from Congress in times of crisis and subsiding to relative inactivity following passage of emergencies. Truman found the traditional presidency unsuited to the new realities, and he moved to make it an instrument of permanent authority and responsibility capable of directing the activities of the nation. During his tenure in the office, Harry S Truman created the contemporary American presidency; by his actions the President was placed at the pinnacle of authority and responsibility in the nation.

Traditionalist views of the presidency have been stated by Truman's predecessors. William Howard Taft held a tightly circumscribed estimation of his duties, best discovered in the title he chose for his volume on the presidency, *Our Chief Magistrate and His Powers* (1925). Taft's definition was strongly legalistic, as befitted a professor of law; he held that the President could exercise no power save that which could be "fairly and reasonably traced to some specific . . . grant in the Federal Constitution or in an act of Congress passed in pursuance thereof." There existed no "undefined residuum" of executive power for Taft.

Theodore Roosevelt saw the presidency as a position from which "the needs of the Nation" could be pressed forward, making use of powers "unless prevented by constitutional or legislative prohibition." In his *Autobiography,* published in 1924, Theodore Roosevelt defined the President as "a steward of the people bound actively and affirmatively to do all he [can] for the people."

Woodrow Wilson applied a more sophisticated analysis to the presidential office, noting the junction of the three presidential roles of legal executive, leader of the nation, and leader of a political party. Because of the "operation of forces inherent in the very nature of government" the President could never again be "a mere executive." "He must stand always at the front of our affairs, and the office will be as big and as influential as the man who occupies it."

Wilson's successors in the office, Harding, Coolidge, and Hoover, proved the truth of Wilson's assertion. Only the disaster of the Great Depression persuaded Hoover of his responsibilities; then he used his presidential powers with little success. Franklin Roosevelt, Truman's traditionalist predecessor, saw the presidency not in terms of administration or engineering (as did Hoover) but as "preeminently a place of moral leadership" which provided "a superb opportunity" for reapplying the traditional rules of morality. From Theodore Roosevelt to Franklin Roosevelt, the incumbents were all concerned with justifying or delimiting the uses of power to serve some vaguely undefined "general welfare" of the nation. All attempted to adopt positions and to take actions designed to ameliorate specific problems, but deep sectional disparities and needs made truly national policies unthinkable.

In direct contrast to his predecessors, Truman insisted that America adopt national policies designed to achieve specific objectives and goals. In setting the national agenda he determined that the nation would work toward two essential purposes: to make "life more worthwhile" for every American and to achieve world peace. Truman was convinced that the nation's prosperity had produced an unequal distribution of wealth; and he was certain that the world need not wage war over resources. In his Fair Deal messages of 1945, 1948, and 1949, Truman restated the frontier radical philosophy espoused by the populists in the 1890s, by William Jennings Bryan in 1896, and by Huey Long in the late 1920s and early 1930s. Truman set forth his program of modern populism, not with the rancor of the old populists, but as the means of assuring social justice in America through intelligent use of the nation's resources. Unlike the old populists, Truman succeeded in engraving frontier radicalism into the bedrock of federal statutory law as the permanent national agenda. In setting this agenda Truman also erected the standard by which he and his successors must be judged.

Since 1945 the President has been the great motivating power of the federal system. Changed conditions coupled with legislative acts which created a new presidential authority in place of the old intermittent presidential powers transformed the President into the embodiment of the nation. Congress has responded to his initiatives, accepting or rejecting his proposals, and on occasion seizing national leadership. The President today is loved or hated but never ignored. It is he who guides his people toward the accomplishment of the national agenda, or he fails in his task. He possesses huge authority and wide responsibility, and he goes far to determine, by his action or inaction, the state of social, political, and economic affairs in America and in the civilized world.

It is the purpose of this study to analyze the creation of the contemporary American presidency, the establishment of the presidential authority, the accomplishments of those who have held the office in modern times, and to indicate some future problems in and prospects for the presidency. No attempt is made to provide encyclopedic information regarding any President; the emphasis lies in the thrust of each administration and its success in achieving the national agenda. There is no intention to produce some artificial model into which each of the incumbents since 1945 may be fitted; nor is there any desire to raise the contemporary American President to national sainthood. This study arises out of recognition that the President of the United States is a central figure in the lives of all who live in the civilized world. Given that the President is such a crucial factor, the chief concern of all is: Who shall be President of the United States?

Old Saybrook, Connecticut
December 1973

1. Hoover and Roosevelt: New Era and New Deal

HERBERT HOOVER: PROPHET OF BUSINESS

The election of 1928 has been subjected to extensive study. The triumph of Herbert C. Hoover over Alfred E. Smith has been variously ascribed to the religious issue, to some final spasmodic effort by which rural America conquered the teeming hordes of the cities, to the moral question posed by Prohibition, and to ethnic voting patterns. Each of these factors contributed to Hoover's overwhelming plurality, but all the issues of 1928 were subsidiary to one question: Who can best continue the nation's prosperity? Early in the campaign Hoover donned the mantle of Business, gathering the great industrial and financial leaders to his bosom and proclaiming his overwhelming faith in America's future. Smith, like William Jennings Bryan in 1908, was reduced to a promise to improve and broaden what already existed. As in 1908, the voters bought the visibly advertised product.

Hoover swept to power on a swell of boundless confidence. Indeed, less than three months before Hoover's inauguration, Calvin Coolidge reported to Congress: "No Congress of the United States ever assembled, on surveying the State of the Union, has met with a more pleasing prospect than that which appears at the present time." Such disparate personalities as Franklin Roosevelt, Walter Lippmann, and Lincoln Steffens solemnly intoned an "Amen." Hoover's victory was an overwhelming indication of the popularity of prosperity. The parent of prosperity was Business; and Hoover was its prophet.

A residue of the old progressivism and the new imperatives of Business were neatly fused in the personality of Herbert Hoover. The new President retained the rhetoric of progressivism while he proclaimed the "ideal of service" so dear to businessmen of the New Era. Certain that the organization known as "the Government" was as susceptible to principles of good business management as any other firm or corporation, Hoover planned an administration truly dedicated "to serve." By extending national unity through the "ideal of service" and through voluntary action of all segments of the American society, Hoover believed the government would become virtually indistinguishable from business. Voluntarism, so effectively employed during Hoover's tenure as Secretary of Commerce, was to be the method and means of his new administration.

Hoover perceived the President of the United States to be chairman of the board of directors of government, which, although unimportant in comparison with Business, could fulfill its proper role by smoothing the way for Business. The entire government would be reorganized to render service to Business, with a guaranteed result of continued and continuing prosperity. Standardization, rationalization, efficiency, an end to wasteful competition, and active governmental cooperation with Business would further boost the productivity of labor. Hoover's prescription was simple: Voluntarism plus efficiency equals increased prosperity.

The words in Hoover's acceptance speech to the Republican convention in 1928 seemed to comprise a mere statement of fact: "Given the chance to go forward with the policies of the last eight years, we shall soon with the help of God be in sight of the day when poverty will be banished from this nation." On March 4, 1929, the new President told the inaugural throng: "I have no fears for the future of our country. It is bright with hope." True, enforcement of Prohibition was not universally successful; the farmer had been forced into a depression by the glut of foods, fats, and fibers; labor unions were appreciably weaker than they had been in 1920; and intellectuals lacked sympathy for the New Era. Nonetheless, most Americans in March 1929 remained fully convinced of infinite wisdom in Calvin Coolidge's summation of national purpose: The business of America is Business.

By common estimate, the country was in good hands. Hoover was a promoter, an engineer, a man of demonstrated administrative ability. Faced with falling farm prices and needed tariff reform, Hoover called a special session of Congress in April 1929. Agreement on action to solve the farm crisis proved elusive, and Hoover resolved to force his own solution. Under considerable presidential pressure, Congress passed legislation to create the Federal Farm Board, a new agency empowered to halt falling prices through "stabilization corporations," with which farmers could cooperate voluntarily. Congress, having expended its energies in the farm fight, recessed in November 1929, leaving the tariff problem untouched.

Hoover as a new President retained Andrew Mellon in his service as Secretary of the Treasury, underscoring his preelection faith in Business as the dynamo of prosperity. Mellon's tax policies in the previous administration had helped to concentrate wealth through increased industrial profits, and in 1929 annual production was rising by huge amounts while competition was sharply curtailed. Between the close of World War I and 1929 the standard of living had surged upward in America while the cost of living had risen only slightly. Hoover, his fellow businessmen, and most in the nation were convinced that prosperity could be maintained indefinitely if Business were permitted to handle its own affairs.

We now know that the prosperity was false. Although corporate profits in 1929 stood at 175 percent of 1922 profits, industrial wages had risen only by about one third in the same period, with surplus assets converted into savings or invested overseas. Speculation in watered stocks, failure to make full use of productive capacity, refusal to share with labor or the consumer the socially desirable portion of the profits generated by more efficient production, investment overseas in financially unsound ventures—all contributed to the ultimate failure. In view of the apparent successes of the economy and the primitive state of economic analysis during the 1920s, it is easy to understand the confidence displayed by most Americans. Granted that the operating units of most public utilities had disappeared into the maw of the great holding companies; granted that a few large organizations dominated mining and manufacturing; granted further that the incomes of the 500 best-paid persons in 1929 equaled the total of all wages paid to production workers in the automobile industry—quarreling with success is always a risky proposition, and few were so inclined in 1929.

Onset of the Great Depression

Hoover had scarcely settled into the White House when he was beset by the great crash of stocks in October 1929. In its wake the President received varying counsel from leading businessmen, financiers, and politicians. Almost none interpreted the crash as the harbinger of general collapse. Only Secretary Mellon seemed to be aware of the threat to general business prosperity, and his advice was Spartan: liquidate labor; liquidate stocks; liquidate the farmer; liqui-

date real estate. Mellon's laissez-faire prescription was far
too harsh for Hoover, and he, a former progressive, rejected
it out-of-hand. The President determined instead to use his
powers of leadership and persuasion to limit the damage
caused by the stock panic. He believed if businessmen continued to expand plants, if businessmen maintained employment, if businessmen bought and sold normally, only the
financial sector would be harmed.

Hoover's method was to persuade the leaders of industry to act as if the stock crash had never occurred. The
effort, if it was to succeed, could not depend solely on a
series of chamber of commerce prayer meetings; voluntarism
required cooperation by both public and private sectors. At
a series of conferences late in 1929 and early in 1930 Hoover
offered the efforts of the entire government in exchange for
Business support of his plan. Business reacted positively to
the President's initiative, and prominent men of affairs
pledged their best efforts to continue operations on a normal
scale. Some marginal enterprise went under, but Business
turned itself to the task of working out its own salvation
under an activist President. In the spring of 1930 the
Hawley-Smoot Tariff, which insulated American industry
from foreign competition by raising the *ad valorem* duty by
50 percent on major imports, became the capstone of the
recovery plan. The formula was fulfilled; prosperity would
be restored by voluntarism and a high protective tariff.

Even as the tariff was passed, the nation settled into
a depression. The spring of 1930 saw over 4,000,000 Americans unemployed, a doubling of the number of families on
relief, and serious curtailment of the workweek and wages.
The nation's economy continued to deteriorate in spite of
Hoover's frequent optimistic statements and the honest
attempts by Business to force recovery. In the public sector
success was equally absent. Although the Farm Board was

able to stabilize wheat prices, farmers producing corn, hogs, beef, and other commodities were wiped out in the price break of early 1930. Hawley-Smoot, by denying the American market to foreign producers, effectively ended the sale of American goods abroad. By election day of 1930 voluntarism was a total and abject failure, especially in its dogmatic refusal to use federal resources to feed the hungry in America.

Autumn of 1930 found the nation in shock. The Democrats, though not fully aware of the potency of the economic issue, campaigned with vigor and captured eight additional seats in the Senate and added fifty-three in the House of Representatives to gain its control. In the Senate, Hoover lost his working majority due to the defeats of conservatives and the presence of progressive Republicans like George W. Norris and Robert M. La Follette, Jr. The Seventy-second Congress, when it convened in December 1931, apparently had few ideas on how to end the depression; Democratic work-relief measures had passed the Seventy-first Congress only to receive the President's veto. Hoover's residual progressivism surfaced again early in 1932, and he made important proposals for congressional action: a Reconstruction Finance Corporation to save businesses and farmers, a public works program to cost some $600,000,000 to $700,000,000, and even a plan to appropriate $300,000,000 to aid the states in poverty relief. He eventually recommended that Congress create a Home Loan Bank to grant federal help to home owners, and he pressed the Federal Reserve System to loosen its lending restrictions.

The legislators, in a surly and fearful mood exacerbated by attacks on the President by Democrats and progressive Republicans, passed what they chose to pass. Congress created the Reconstruction Finance Corporation only to find that its loans went largely to Republican-owned banks; under severe pressure from the banking lobby it fatally weakened the Home Loan Bank System; it refused Hoover's initiative on public works and reenacted virtually the same Garner-Wagner Relief Bill which Hoover had vetoed in 1931. To add to the confusion, Hoover took direct action to cut the expenditures of the executive branch, thus precipitating increased unemployment.

In the spring of 1932 a "bonus army," made up of veterans who wanted and needed payment of a World War I bonus promised to them by Congress over the President's veto, moved into Washington, D.C. Hoover perceived a threat of bolshevism in this act, and he ordered the United States Army to disperse the bonus-seekers. General Douglas MacArthur, with Dwight D. Eisenhower and George S. Patton, made short work of the bonus army in the "Battle of the Anacostia Mud Flats." The President's popularity reached a new low. By summer 1932, farm prices had fallen so low that the Farm Holiday Association sponsored massive resistance to farm foreclosures and successfully blocked the delivery of farm commodities to market. The movement affected nineteen states, most of them in the Middle Border.

By 1932 Hoover was a bewildered man, numbed by his failure, with the stench of conspiracy in his nostrils. As early as 1931 he believed the source of the Great Depression to be outside the United States. As the months passed, the President reverted to his basic economic credo: Balance the budget, and financial stability must follow. He was genuinely disturbed when the economy failed to respond to his remedies, for he saw the system as basically sound, needing only an adjustment of some particular part or component which was causing the machine to sputter. He worked harder than ever before, and his inability to solve his problem by managerial means left him bereft of other solutions. It is important for us to realize that few Americans, except those of the radical left or right, saw any need for government intervention in the economy. In every other panic in United States' history the economy had adjusted itself; the panic of 1930 to 1932 was thought to be no different.

The Election of 1932

As the election of 1932 approached, Hoover saw himself as the beleaguered champion of Business and of the entire tradition of individualism in America. His progressive leanings were finally cast aside, and he became more conservative and ideological as the grim days passed. The ceremonial trappings of the White House, the increased detail of Secret Service agents, the endless concerts of the Marine Band, the substitution of press releases for press conferences, and Hoover's heightened concern with bolshevism and its attacks on the American way of life betrayed his view of the world. The President determined to save the nation from itself by running for reelection. The Republican convention of 1932 was a drab affair, carefully organized to renominate Herbert Hoover and to put forward his program as its platform. In the only contest of the convention, the Prohibition plank in the platform was changed, in a way guaranteed to offend both "wets" and "drys." In the summer of 1932, with notable lack of enthusiasm, Republicans renominated the hero of 1928.

Hoover's campaign centered on the "three cornerstones" of his policy: defending the gold standard of payments, preserving the high protective tariff, and maintaining the balanced budget. Even in the face of the obvious failure of these remedies, he clung doggedly to his economic principles. In the Republican heartland of Nebraska and the Dakotas, the President spoke to these points only to be greeted by apathy or catcalls from his hearers. In a few places he was greeted with enthusiasm or outspoken hatred; in most places the smell of failure accompanied his tour. Yet it appears that Hoover was not too disheartened by his reception and that he counted on Business to assure his reelection.

By the end of summer, however, the President was beginning to perceive his rival, Franklin D. Roosevelt, as a dangerous radical. Following Roosevelt's strong showing in Maine in September 1932, Hoover launched an energetic campaign based on his fears for the future of the nation. The tack was entirely unworthy of Hoover, but in his frustration and desperation, he had convinced himself that Roosevelt was a dangerous man who espoused an alien philosophy of government. As Hoover wound up his campaign in Madison Square Garden, he warned against the new radicals. He intoned the roster: Cutting, Hearst, Long, La Follette, Wheeler, Norris, and Roosevelt—all of them dedicated to the destruction of America's values. Hoover's summary of the lone issue was apocalyptic: "This election is not a mere shift from the ins to the outs. It means deciding the direction our Nation will take over a century to come." On election day the voters repudiated Hoover; only six northeastern states gave him their electoral votes, and Roosevelt outpolled the President by 22,800,000 votes to Hoover's 15,800,000. Not since 1912 had an incumbent President been so thoroughly humiliated.

Evaluation of Hoover's Presidency

How shall we evaluate the presidency of Herbert Hoover? Was he a mere victim of circumstance, who happened to be President when the Great Depression struck? Was he immobilized by ideology at a moment which demanded activism? Did he "just stand around" and do nothing? The answers to these questions have long been confounded. Hoover was an experienced administrator long before he entered the White House, and too much credence has been attached to Louis Howe's quip that Hoover was the great engineer who "dammed, ditched, and drained the country in the period of three short years." Hoover was a qualified mining engineer, but his reputation and wealth had been made as a promoter of enterprise, as a "new breed" manager who moved head-on to diagnose deficiencies and adopt remedies for problems. His poise and self-control in the face of the stock panic go too often unnoticed, and his rejection of Mellon's advice to liquidate everything and everybody offers some gauge of Hoover's willingness to face his task, the task of discovering and rectifying the conditions which prevented prosperity from continuing. Even his morose reaction to events of 1931 and 1932 may be traced more properly to his feeling that others were losing the "true faith" than to any self-doubt.

Hoover failed as President precisely because he was unable to question the principles and methods which had always in the past proved workable for him. His earlier progressivism motivated him to assume an activist presidency, while his experience with voluntarism during his years at Commerce led him to accept self-help and the cooperation of Business and government as the "sovereign remedy." In sum, he sought a short-term cure for a short-term malady. He was willing to aid the industrialist, the businessman, the farmer, and the home owner; eventually he came around to supporting a huge public works program and to granting needed aid to the states to meet their relief crisis. But he confined his role to that of diagnostician rather than healer of the nation. His concern for the nation was couched not in the ineffective specifics of his policy but became misplaced in the generalities of individualism and collectivism which he voiced at the close of the campaign of 1932. The voters reacted by placing on Hoover the sins and failures of Business and by driving him into the political desert.

Hoover's final months in the presidency produced further evidence of the nation's economic crisis. Businesses continued to fail; banks closed their doors; jobless totals soared; and hunger claimed its victims in America. In a desperate attempt to mount some attack on the Great Depression, Hoover called upon President-elect Franklin D. Roosevelt to join in assuming responsibility for what Hoover might do to alleviate conditions. During the long months from election day to March 4, 1933, Roosevelt refused to accept any of the burden of the presidential office, arguing quite properly that he had no official standing and that he could not be bound by Hoover's last efforts.

FRANKLIN D. ROOSEVELT: EMERGENCY PROGRAMS

What Roosevelt was not saying was that he had few better ideas for coping with the crisis. He was a product of Hoover's generation; he brought to the presidency the same simplistic economics possessed by Hoover; and his platform offered the same economic remedies which had already failed Hoover: the balanced budget and heavy slashes in federal expenditures. It was obvious, though never explicitly stated, that Roosevelt would consult the same oracles, utter the same incantations, divine the same entrails, and conquer the Great Depression. In an era which produced forceful and effective leadership in Germany, Italy, and Russia, many bewildered Americans were seeking a great leader. The nation was ready in 1933 to be molded by the style and personality of the new leader.

Roosevelt's first words as President were chosen to reinstall confidence in the ability of Americans to solve their own problems. The inaugural address rang with expressions of faith in traditional American means of achieving success: clear and unblinking recognition of the crisis, willingness to work, reform of the inequities and injustices of the national life. The rhetoric was that of the old progressives as Roosevelt reaffirmed his faith in the perfectibility of man; good must triumph over evil. The assignment was difficult, the tasks severe and onerous, but Franklin Roosevelt would defend traditional American democracy and the American enterprise system of production.

The most frequently quoted line of the inaugural, "We have nothing to fear but fear itself," is not only meaningless but has obscured the tenor of the address. The President's remarks bristled with bellicose language and descriptions. He spoke of the American people "moving as a trained and loyal army willing to sacrifice for the good of a common discipline." He saw fit to "assume unhesitatingly the leadership of this great army of our people dedicated to a disciplined attack upon our common problem." He would not, said the President, evade a "temporary departure from our normal balance of [executive and congressional] public procedure." Should the other branches of government prove unable to cooperate in the attack on the Great Depression, Roosevelt would "ask the Congress for the one remaining instrument to meet the crisis—broad Executive power to wage a war against the emergency, as great as the power that would be given to me if we were in fact invaded by a foreign foe." Roosevelt's first inaugural was no lullaby. Its language was that of the 1930s: harsh, bellicose, and demanding obedience in support of firm leadership. The speech promised action but gave no hint regarding plans or programs.

Roosevelt's first three months in office became known as the Hundred Days, an era of cooperation between President and Congress unprecedented in peacetime. The Hundred Days were filled with emergency legislation which extended federal aid to business, farmers, homeowners, the unemployed, youth, the starving and homeless, and to cities and towns through the "alphabet agencies" of the New Deal. It is ironic but understandable that the first to be buoyed up by the new federal relief programs was the banking industry, rescued by the Emergency Banking Act of 1933, which was written while dancers attended Roosevelt's inaugural ball. Congress, the enemy of Hoover, played a faithful role as rubber stamp to the flood of bills from the White House; and Republicans and Democrats alike vied to be first to support the President's next move.

The new President was, meanwhile, taking no chances on congressional reluctance or revolt. Within a few weeks of taking office he began a series of "fireside chats" with the American people which took him by radio into the homes of the nation. His mellifluous voice, simple delivery, unmistakable accent, and clear explanations of his major projects built a base of popular support that Congress dared not challenge. Roosevelt's self-confidence, his compassion for those bearing the misery of the depression, and his willingness to lead toward the future pervaded the nation. The miracle of radio, in the hands of a man who outperformed the radio "professionals" and took delight in it, unified the nation in a surge of "shared direction" of federal affairs. The political apathy so characteristic of the 1920s was gone, to be replaced by an explosion of nationalism among people who had never before felt they had any role in government, those who were to come out in 1936, 1940, and 1944 to elect and reelect Roosevelt President for life.

The New Deal was, at base, an era of moral regeneration, and many of Roosevelt's fireside chats were actually sermons. The President retained most of his progressive values throughout his tenure, including his desire for a sound dollar and his discomfort in the presence of an unbalanced budget. Roosevelt was a reluctant "big spender." He refused to devalue the dollar until he found that a group of old populists, led by Senator Burton K. Wheeler of Montana, had nearly enough votes in the Senate to enact the Populist party plank of 1892 and require coinage of silver at a ratio of sixteen to one with gold. Although on paper Roosevelt maintained a single administrative budget of income and expenditures, he was able, in his mind, to separate the costs of "regular government" from "emergency programs." The idea of "emergency funding" for "emergency problems" permitted the President to hold down the costs of "normal government" while he maintained his belief that huge "emergency spending" would terminate with the end of the crisis. Throughout his tenure Roosevelt demanded a balanced budget, and the recession of 1937 can be traced directly to the decrease in federal spending needed to achieve the budget balance in 1937.

Cornerstones of the New Deal

Roosevelt went far beyond progressivism in his willingness to experiment. Indeed, the New Deal's reputation for innovation rests largely on three enactments, of which only one proved permanent. The three, the Agricultural Adjustment Act of 1933, the National Industrial Recovery Act, and the Tennessee Valley Act, form the cornerstones of the New Deal experiments. Neither the AAA nor the NIRA ever received Roosevelt's unlimited support. The AAA was founded on a series of recommendations by farm leaders called to the White House in 1933 and led in conference by the visionary Secretary of Agriculture, Henry A. Wallace. The new law, which was essentially an updated version of the populist subtreasury plan of 1892, consolidated mortgage and rural credit aid to farmers and directed the President to take action to raise farm prices to parity with the golden era of American agriculture, 1909–1914. Restrictions on meat production, limitations on acreage to be planted, and purchasing agreements designed to raise the prices of farm commodities were exempted from the antitrust laws. Funds for the operations of the act would come from "processing taxes" laid on the middlemen who transformed, packaged, or processed farm products. The original AAA was struck down by the Supreme Court in January 1936, and new farm legislation was required in 1936 and again in 1938.

The National Industrial Recovery Act was an attempt to do for industry and labor what was being done for the farmer by AAA. Like the agricultural legislation, NIRA permitted "floor prices" to be set for goods; firms could divide up the various markets; and each industry was allowed to adopt its own production code which set standards for manufacturers. While industry was given the right to monopolize markets in the cause of higher prices, labor was guaranteed the right to organize. Minimum wages for labor and limitations on the workweek were expected to increase both wages and employment. All activities undertaken by industry and labor under the NIRA were subject to "codes" approved by government and exempted from the antitrust laws. Although the NIRA legislation was introduced by liberal Democrat Hugo L. Black of Alabama and appeared to be a major intervention in the economy by government, the act was largely permissive. In spite of a massive publicity campaign and the adoption of a stylized blue eagle as its symbol, the NIRA was a simple device to raise prices by eliminating competition. By the time NIRA was declared unconstitutional in 1935, the blue eagle, the production codes, and the famous charter of labor in Section 7A had done little except to aid Big Business. Only its labor provisions were reenacted into law by the New Deal.

The TVA, which was at once the most important social experiment and the most violently opposed project of the Roosevelt administration, became a permanent monument to the experimentation of the Roosevelt era. The Tennessee Valley Authority Act took the people, social structure, resources, and geography of an entire river system and transformed them through governmental activity into a new and important entity in the nation. TVA was socialism, pure and simple; TVA was unique in that Franklin Roosevelt never wavered in his commitment to the success of the experiment. But TVA was not the brainchild of Roosevelt, Moley, Lillienthal, or any other New Dealer; rather, it was the result of an idea and of a willingness to support this idea for more than a decade by the progressive Republican from Nebraska, Senator George W. Norris. In its insistence on the use of public money, in its attack on established public utilities, in its decision to flood huge parcels of land which had supported towns and homes, in its firm commitment to planned development, and in its capacity to engage in protracted lobbying and open battle against its enemies, the TVA was actually the antithesis of the ever-shifting, pragmatic New Deal.

Roosevelt's involvement with the TVA began even before his inauguration. Touring the valley with Norris, Roosevelt envisioned a broader development of electrical power as a means of social uplift, flood control, improved land use, and installation of industry in an area of stark economic deprivation. The adoption of Norris's proposal was so complete, the transmission of Roosevelt's message on TVA to Congress so rapid, and passage of the bill so precipitate that TVA emerged in the midst of the flood of emergency measures. It was perhaps the only way in which a successful fight for public power could be waged. Whether or not the TVA was truly a part of the New Deal, it partook of Franklin Roosevelt's vision of social and economic uplift of disadvantaged people. TVA remains even today Roosevelt's greatest monument.

Conservatism of the New Deal

Antitrust activity of the Department of Justice, often taken as a measure of the progressive nature of an administration, was infrequent and of low pressure throughout the New Deal. Although it was apparent to the casual observer that concentration of wealth had accompanied the rationalization of industry and transportation in the 1920s, the problems of the Great Depression required conscious efforts to raise prices, efforts which could only be helped by monopolistic competition. It is no accident that the AAA and the NIRA had in common exemptions from the prohibitions of the antitrust laws. The 1939 investigation by Congress into economic concentration led only to publication in 1941 of the *Report of the Temporary National Economic Committee.* By the time of the report, the climate had grown unfriendly to antitrust efforts, since war production demanded that monopolies and oligopolies be permitted to survive and produce on cost-plus contracts. New Deal rhetoric against the power of corporations was overwhelming; New Deal activity was lacking.

The New Deal was attacked by its enemies as a planned assault on capitalism and as an attempt to regiment America in the service of socialism. What went unrecognized was that the New Deal was without a plan, and in spite of the efforts of Tugwell and others to bring some structure to the New Deal programs, Roosevelt failed to set a truly rational policy. His closest approach to a rational overview of national purpose came in a 1932 campaign speech to the Commonwealth Club of San Francisco, in which the candidate declared that the government "owes to everyone an avenue to possess himself of a portion of that plenty [produced by the national economy] sufficient for his own needs, through his own work." Taken in the context of the speech, Roosevelt's words indicated no intention to redistribute wealth in the nation, although he did make vague references to planning the economy. Given the economic analysis commonly practiced by Americans in 1932, it would be fatuous to think Roosevelt should have been more prescient than professional economists of his era. In short, the New Deal had no coherent plan, much less an intellectual commitment to redistributing wealth through economic planning.

The New Deal reforms were essentially revisions of progressive ideas. The Securities Exchange Act of 1934 tried to drive dishonesty from the securities markets. The Public Utilities Holding Company Act was designed to end excessive rates imposed on users of electric power by artificially inflated costs. The Merchant Marine Act of 1936 was a curious amalgam of nationalism, relief, and make-work for shipyards and maritime labor. Even the National Labor Relations Act and the Social Security Act must be seen as long overdue measures to obtain for Americans rights and protections which had even existed in Bismarck's German Empire before 1890.

The New Deal was largely an extension of the personality of Roosevelt and the charismatic leadership he was able to exert in the economic crisis. From 1933 to 1945 Roosevelt dominated the national attention and created the national mood with his incessant activity, his calls for national unity, his countless new projects, his novel approaches to old problems, and his unparalleled ability to relate to Americans on an individual basis. To turn the McLuhan phrase, the message was the medium. The New Deal, in the person of Roosevelt, constantly preached, advocated, exhorted, and enacted programs which demonstrated the vitality of America. Where the New Deal succeeded, Roosevelt succeeded; where Roosevelt failed, the New Deal failed. To separate Roosevelt from the New Deal is impossible. He was at once the architect, the chief experimenter, the ringleader, the father image, the good neighbor (and his enemies thought he saw himself as the Good Shepherd), and the true-blue American. He was a progressive whose failure as businessman and investor had immunized him against the charm of Business. He went well beyond the limitations which earlier progressives had placed on themselves. He forced himself to cooperate with Labor, allowing only a few lapses; he cleared his mind of the notion that the poor are poor only because they won't work; he purged himself of the antiseptic "do-goodism" which had made progressives distasteful; and he successfully appealed to minority groups as one who cared for them.

Effects of the New Deal

By 1939 the mood of the country had been immeasurably improved by the New Deal's myriad of programs, projects, and proposals. The size of the federal establishment had more than tripled, and the evident federal intervention in national life convinced people that the New Deal was taking hold. But the specific facts of the national economy belie any such interpretation. From 1933 to 1939 unemployment never fell below 9,000,000; some 2,750,000 young men were held out of the labor market by service in the Civilian Conservation Corps; and the six years of experimentation before

World War II left the rural poor, both white and black, virtually untouched by permanent programs. The New Deal was not devoted to remaking the nation; it was an attempt to relieve the crisis, remove the abuses which had set off the depression, and restore the old values. When war came to Europe in 1939, that conflagration set off a boom in America which erased the need for further relief.

Roosevelt was the last of the traditional Presidents and, in part, the transitional figure who preceded the first contemporary American President. His intent to restore traditional values was a constant theme of his speeches, and he made no attempt during his tenure to question the accepted ideals of modified capitalism and limited popular control of government which had marked America in the first two decades of this century. Even the Wealth Tax Act of 1935, hailed as a radical proposal, did not foresee a massive redistribution of wealth in America. At the time the act was passed, some 13.4 percent of all income received in the nation had gone to the top one percent of the population; by the time of entry into World War II the same one percent still received 11.5 percent of the national income. Even the heavy taxation of World War II, which redistributed wealth to an unprecedented degree, was designed primarily to pay for the war and to "sop up" excess purchasing power which threatened wartime price controls.

Nor did the New Deal consciously attempt to widen the franchise by bringing in minority group voters. The number of workers who voted, particularly those who were members of politically active labor unions, increased throughout the period of the New Deal, but at that time few restrictions were placed on the opportunity of industrial workers to vote in the states in which they lived. The New Dealers were sensitive to the deprivations under which most minorities lived, and the President supported relief programs to ease the plight of less fortunate Americans. Yet no serious proposals were made by the administration to extend the vote to poor whites, Negroes, or Mexican-Americans in areas where the poll tax insured effective political control in the hands of the more affluent. The New Deal coalition, made up of the "solid South," urban voters, discontented farmers, and organized labor, continued its hold on the nation without enfranchising new groups. From the pragmatic viewpoint there was no sense in antagonizing southern Democrats to seek the votes of the southern poor, which were not needed in any case to reelect the President. The New Dealers were extremely practical in the matter of reelection.

Conditions within the executive branch of government under the New Deal disclosed no persistent attempt to reorganize the bureaucracy. Except where corruption or incompetence were rampant, the executive agencies were permitted to conduct their business, with "emergency agencies" being created to take "emergency action" during the crisis. In an unconscious anticipation of the "competitive management" scheme so successfully employed by General Motors in the 1950s, Roosevelt blithely parceled out powers and responsibilities in his attack on the Great Depression. Although formal control of the Public Works Administration was given to Harold Ickes's Department of the Interior, the huge supply of money was allotted to the "emergency" Federal Emergency Relief Administration, headed by Harry Hopkins. Hopkins also ran the Works Progress Administration which created far more public works than Ickes was willing to tolerate. NRA authorized an ambitious public works plan, but its direction was given to Ickes rather than to the NRA administrator, General Hugh Johnson. From start to finish the New Deal was an administrative wilderness inhabited by predatory bureaucrats who eyed hungrily each appropriation of funds.

The overlappings of authority, the assignment of two or sometimes three agencies to operate in a single area on the same problem, and the lack of clear lines of organizational power failed to cripple the New Deal. The President kept things constantly on the move. Always smiling, always optimistic, always prodding, always seeking more action, always asking more than an individual could contribute in time and effort, always unwilling to discipline or fire an incompetent, Roosevelt kept finding more things to be done. The key to success in every venture, he assured all, was high hope and a thirst for accomplishment. But Roosevelt never moved beyond a conservative view of the role of government in America. Roosevelt's most comprehensive statement of governmental purpose was made in the 1932 Commonwealth Club speech. His phrases contained no radical prescription for the nation:

> *Government includes the art of formulating a policy, and using the political technique to attain so much of that policy as will receive public support; persuading, leading, sacrificing, teaching always, because the greatest duty of a statesman is to educate . . . We must build toward a time when a major depression cannot occur again; and if this means sacrificing the easy profits of inflationary booms, then let them go; and good riddance.*

As President, Roosevelt undoubtedly fulfilled many of the goals he had set for himself as a young progressive. Little that needed reforming escaped his ministrations, but Roosevelt confined himself to reform. His view of the presidency limited him to a posture of defending the old values of a national prosperity in which most Americans shared and defending a democratic government controlled by those citizens who traditionally voted. His last progressive victories came in 1938 and 1939, when he obtained passage of the

Agricultural Adjustment Act of 1938, the Fair Labor Standards Act of 1939, and the Executive Reorganization Act of 1939. By 1938, when the recession of 1937 had been stemmed by resumed federal spending, a conservative coalition of northern Republicans and southern Democrats had come together to prevent further reform. The coalition, resulting from the President's uncharacteristic lapse of political acumen during the "court packing" fight of 1937, successfully blunted the New Deal antitrust drive of 1939 and limited its effect to a mere publication of the *Report of the TNEC,* as noted above.

Evaluation of Roosevelt's Presidency

How shall we evaluate the presidency of Franklin D. Roosevelt? Roosevelt possessed, in exactly the proper mix, a patrician disdain for the newly rich and a willingness to serve as champion for the average American. He was the charismatic leader best suited to Americans, not only in time of crisis but probably also in less arduous days. Many Americans secretly look for a king, and Roosevelt appeared, to many of his countrymen, to be a constitutional monarch deeply concerned for the nation. He was different from his subjects (as a good king should be) in family background, education, attitude toward the powerful, and in his unselfish devotion to the welfare of his people. He offered the nation an example of a man who had conquered adversity through his own will, and he displayed unending restless energy cloaked in urbane rhetoric and an irresistible spirit of good humor. The President was entirely credible to the voters who elected him President for life, and for most Americans he was not only "Mr. President" but also "His Most Democratic Majesty."

Roosevelt was a successful President because he addressed himself to matters at hand, refusing no possible remedy, certain that divine Providence had surely guided the hand of the voters. He was able to pass on to his successor a nation whose political and economic processes had been repaired, a nation which had successfully waged the greatest war in recorded history, and a nation ready to assume world leadership at the same moment it dedicated itself to an innovative course at home.

COMPARISON OF HOOVER AND ROOSEVELT

The chief difference between Hoover and Roosevelt lay in temperament. Both were defensive in their outlooks and sought means of defending traditional American values. Both made limited analyses of their problems and adopted remedies which were ill-defined and sometimes at odds with other palliatives already being administered. Because of the poor state of economic analysis in their era, both Hoover and Roosevelt failed to understand what was taking place, and they responded to each crisis on an *ad hoc* basis, thus foreclosing any possibility of adopting truly national policy. Both were willing, and Roosevelt was eager, to espouse activist solutions to the Great Depression, but neither sought or obtained a clear view of the national purpose.

Both Hoover and Roosevelt were traditional American Presidents, because they held office in a time when the nation was divided by sectionalism, when industrial activity was largely confined to the North and the West Coast, when the South lay in economic and cultural peonage to the other sections, and when there existed no self-conscious identification by Americans as being different from other people. Both Hoover and Roosevelt served at a time when the melting pot had not quite performed its task, when industry had risen but had not yet extended its blessings and burdens to the entire country, when people in Georgia looked with suspicion on the cars from New York which bore the "Yankees" southward to Florida, and when Boston was the cultural capital of the nation.

Hoover and Roosevelt were traditional Presidents in traditional times, before the nation had been unified in the crucible of World War II. They were the last of their breed, the last to deal with problems which differed in nature depending on their point of origin. Both underwent experiences during their tenures which foreshadowed the future role of the contemporary American President. Hoover, had he recognized it, was engaged in a national struggle to restore the economy, but his horizon was limited to the business community as the sole source of prosperity. Roosevelt confined himself to relief measures and necessary reforms in banking, finance, social security, and unemployment insurance. It is ironic that Roosevelt, genuinely a man of peace, achieved his greatest success in national unification during World War II. The military experience of 13,000,000 Americans, a truly national draft law, the tearing away of whole populations from their settled locations to aid the war effort, and the sharp increase in racial self-consciousness among minority groups were all products of the war.

Where Hoover failed, Roosevelt succeeded. Where Hoover was goaded to near paranoia regarding the dedication of his fellow citizens to the "old values," Roosevelt successfully defended them. Where Hoover was unable to adapt to changed conditions, Roosevelt became the author of change. Where Hoover was a prisoner of events, Roosevelt fitted events into a pliable mold called the New Deal. Where

Hoover's progressivism gave way to the philosophy of New Era Business, Roosevelt's progressivism was transmogrified into a liberalism which rid itself of the antiseptic smugness which had doomed progressivism as a movement. Liberalism, through its inclusionist tendencies, was able to attract and enlist a great voting coalition of old progressives, ethnic groups, discontented farmers, and workers in the support and service of the New Deal. Unlike progressivism, liberalism sought to do for people what they wanted done more than to do what was right for people. As a result, liberalism was less disciplined than was progressivism, but liberalism was decidedly more popular and flexible as a means of political action. Roosevelt, as the founder of liberalism, demonstrated that extremist solutions were not necessary to the survival of America and her traditional values during the Great Depression.

NOTES

The 1920s: The flavor of the 1920s is best portrayed in the lively and impressionistic account by Frederick Lewis Allen, *Only Yesterday* (1931). William E. Leuchtenberg, *The Perils of Prosperity* (1958), offers a compelling interpretation of the overwhelming acceptance of Business by Americans in the 1920s and the conflict of country versus city in that era.

Evaluation of Hoover: Hoover's evaluation of his own presidency is in his *Memoirs* (1951, two volumes), while the best recent study of the Hoover policies is H. G. Warren, *Herbert Hoover and the Great Depression* (1959).

1928 Election: Highly perceptive of the religious issue in the election of 1928 is E. A. Moore's *A Catholic Runs for President* (1956), while Samuel Lubell, *The Future of American Politics* (1952), espouses the urban revolt thesis.

The Great Depression: John Kenneth Galbraith's *The Great Crash* (1955) is a witty and highly readable account of the coming of the Great Depression and the reactions of Hoover and the leaders of business to the calamity.

1932 Election: Frank Freidel, *Franklin D. Roosevelt: The Triumph* (1956), provides an excellent account of the election of 1932, as do R. V. Peel and T. C. Donnelly in *The 1932 Campaign* (1935).

"Emergency": The use of the term "emergency" was commonplace throughout the New Deal, indicating that the President and his advisers fully expected to see the demise of the abnormal conditions and the "emergency agencies" and the restoration of the old prosperity.

FDR and the New Deal: Tomes on Franklin Roosevelt and the New Deal have become a national cottage industry for scholars and journalists alike. Arthur M. Schlesinger, Jr.'s "Age of Roosevelt" has reached three volumes: *The Crisis of the Old Order* (1957), *The Coming of the New Deal* (1959), and *The Politics of Upheaval* (1960). Frank Freidel has published three volumes of his biography "Franklin Roosevelt": *The Apprenticeship* (1952), *The Ordeal* (1954), and *The Triumph* (1956). The best single-volume treatment of the era is William E. Leuchtenberg's *Franklin D. Roosevelt and the New Deal* (1963). James M. Burns's *Roosevelt: The Lion and the Fox* (1956) attempts to explain the complicated character and psychology of Roosevelt. That "remote psychoanalysis" is not yet out of style may be seen from James Barber's *The Presidential Character* (1972).

Critics of FDR: For the attacks on Roosevelt by conservatives, see George Wolfskill, *The Revolt of the Conservatives: A History of the American Liberty League* (1962). Left-oriented onslaughts are the subject of Donald McCoy's *Angry Voices: Left-of-Center Politics in the New Deal Era* (1958). The activities of the radio priest Father Charles E. Coughlin are explained and analyzed in Charles J. Tull, *Father Coughlin and the New Deal* (1965). Carl Degler,

Out of Our Past (1959), sees the New Deal as a major effort to establish a "guarantor state" capable of providing some minimum guarantee of well-being for all. If the New Deal was a "guarantor," its guarantee was at least as anemic as that of earlier progressives; T. Harry Williams, *Huey Long* (1969), provides an excellent study of the Louisiana populist and his program.

Progressives and the New Deal: For differing views on the contributions of the old progressives to the New Deal, see Otis L. Graham, *An Encore for Reform: The Old Progressives and the New Deal* (1967), and Richard Hofstadter, *The Age of Reform* (1955), who views the New Deal as a "drastic new departure . . . in the history of American reformism," (p. 302). See also, Thomas K. McCraw, *TVA and the Power Fight, 1933–1939* (1971).

Commonwealth Club Speech: The complete Commonwealth Club Speech is reprinted in Samuel I. Rosenman, editor, *The Public Papers and Addresses of Franklin D. Roosevelt (1938–1950)*, vol. 1, pp. 742–746.

A Unified U.S.: Richard Polenberg's *War and Society* (1972) details the emergence of the newly unified nation at the end of World War II as "the end of an old era and the beginning of a new," (author's prologue, p. 4).

2. Harry S Truman: The Fair Deal

On the death of a British monarch, the cry goes up, "The King is dead; long live the King." No such words of continuity were heard on April 13, 1945, when Franklin Roosevelt died. The nation's best-loved man, the true American monarch the citizens preferred above all others by electing him President for life, the leader who personified the hopes of his fellow Americans was dead. Within three hours, as provided in the Constitution, Vice-President Harry S Truman took the oath of office as thirty-third President of the United States. Given the times, the circumstances, and people's emotions, no American then living could have actually replaced Franklin D. Roosevelt. There was no new king.

The new President was a serious man. He was no great orator smoothly evoking images of peace and prosperity, and he had no national constituency. The public erred in its assessment of Truman, seeing the eagle replaced by a sparrow, the king giving way to a mere commoner. Americans wallowed in self-pity and sorrowing misjudgment, misjudgment made believable both by appearances and national inclinations. The nation identified its new President only as the Missouri politician selected by Roosevelt to be his running mate in 1944. Truman himself added to this attitude by declaring his feeling that "the moon, the stars, and all the planets" had fallen on him.

EARLY CAREER OF
HARRY S TRUMAN

Harry Truman attended the public schools of Independence, Missouri and graduated from high school in 1901. He held various minor jobs in Independence and Kansas City until 1906, when he returned to the family farm at Blue Ridge, Missouri. On Flag Day 1905, when Battery B of the Missouri National Guard was formed at Independence, Harry Truman became a charter member of the unit and privately indulged a part of his earlier desire to attend the United States Military Academy, a wish unfulfilled due to his poor eyesight. In 1908 he joined the Masonic Lodge of Belton, Missouri, and three years later he organized a new Masonic group, Grandview Lodge, No. 618. After service in World War I, he formed a partnership with his friend Eddie Jacobson and opened a haberdashery in Kansas City but fell victim to the recession of 1921. Truman's creditors tried to force him into bankruptcy, but he refused the relief offered by the bankruptcy law. Eventually, he repaid every cent owed to suppliers and bankers alike.

Truman entered politics in 1921 through his friendship with Jim Pendergast, a fellow artillery officer and nephew of the notorious machine politician, Tom Pendergast. It was largely through the support of the Pendergast machine of Kansas City that Truman won a narrow primary nomination for judge of eastern Jackson County. He was victorious in the election of 1922 and thus began his first service as a public administrator. But Truman's bid for reelection was swept away in a bitter primary fight in 1924, and he subsequently took a job selling memberships in the Kansas City Auto Club, tried his hand in a savings and loan association, and reorganized a bank which had failed. He was active in the army reserve, and in 1921 he organized Missouri Chapter 1 of the Reserve Officers Association.

A surface appraisal of Truman's career to 1924 marks him a failure in almost every venture. A more thorough assessment reveals that Truman possessed major abilities in originating, organizing, and selling ideas. By 1924 his active Masonic membership had brought him election as deputy grand master of the Fifty-ninth District, Missouri Masons, and he regularly attended meetings of the Grand Lodge of Missouri. During his brief, involuntary retirement from politics he also built his ties with the voters of Jackson County and won election as presiding judge in 1926.

As presiding judge, Truman was to administer the largest and richest county of Missouri, but on taking office he found that the county buildings had been long neglected, that the county roads had been cheaply built, and that the county was far deeper in debt than he had realized. Worse, the county bonds held by banks in Kansas City carried annual interest at a rate of 6 percent. Truman quietly obtained alternate financing in Chicago and Saint Louis at an annual rate of 4 percent at first, later at 2.5 percent per year. In 1927 he received voter approval for a bond issue of $6,500,000 and, the following year, an additional $8,500,000 in bonding authority. The money was spent on a new highway system for Jackson County, rebuilding courthouses at Independence and Kansas City, and a new hospital at the county home at Little Blue, Missouri.

During his campaign for election to this office, Truman had spelled out his plan for county construction contracts, then notorious in Missouri as a source of graft. All work would be put out for competitive bidding; the bids would be publicly opened at a prescribed time; and the contract would be awarded to the lowest bidder. A bipartisan board of engineers would inspect the contracted work at various stages of completion, and no payment would be made for projects which did not fulfill specifications. Following the election, when the first contracts were to be let, Tom Pendergast invited Truman to a meeting with several of Pendergast's contractor "friends." Truman attended the meeting, told Pendergast that contracts would be awarded exactly as he had promised the voters, and received no further overtures from Pendergast's friends. Pendergast not only admired Truman's direct stand but took comfort in the knowledge that there was sufficient business for himself and his friends in the boom of 1927 and 1928.

Truman's administration of Jackson County between 1926 and 1934 entailed the handling and spending of more than $60,000,000. During that period he supervised the planning and construction of a county road system compatible with the new state system, reformed the tax structure, and left the county virtually without debt. In 1928 Truman also organized the Greater Kansas City Regional Planning Organization, an association which provided the advantage of professional planning for the county and brought him into intimate contact with other county judges and the "courthouse gangs" of the entire state.

In 1934, on the basis of his outstanding administrative record, Truman planned to run for Congress from the new Fourth Congressional District, which included eastern Jackson County. This new district also promptly drew the attention of two experienced congressmen. In addition, Truman found that the Pendergast machine was already committed to a candidate for the new seat but had no one to back against incumbent United States Senator Roscoe C. Patterson, who was seeking reelection on the Republican ticket. Truman entered the senatorial primary and combined his Kansas City support with a campaign waged statewide by the "courthouse gangs" he knew so well. His Masonic and veterans memberships also formed a solid part of his political base. He won the Democratic nomination by a narrow margin, and in November 1934, Truman defeated Senator Patterson by over 750,000 votes.

POLITICAL METHODS AND PHILOSOPHY

On January 3, 1935, when Truman took the oath of office, he brought to the United States Senate both a political method and a developed political philosophy. His experience was that of a self-taught public administrator who saw government as a powerful tool designed to solve problems and obtain results. The proper result could be assured, he was convinced, by careful study of the question at hand, by thorough analysis of proposed remedies, and by arriving at a decision on a coldly analytical basis. The foundation of the analysis was formed by political reality, but honest appraisal and strict financial accountability were essential to success.

Truman's political philosophy was an amalgam of ideas drawn from four major sources. First, his complete loyalty to the Democratic party arose from his family roots in Shelby County, Kentucky and the devotion of his Confederate ancestors to the Old Democracy. Second, his father, John Anderson Truman, was a rabid Democrat who approved and followed the leadership of William Jennings Bryan as the Democratic party was recast in the populist mold. Harry Truman was attracted to progressivism and sympathized with Theodore Roosevelt, although he waited for Woodrow Wilson to advance the New Freedom before giving his vote to the progressive movement. By 1932 County Judge Truman was actively campaigning for Franklin D. Roosevelt, and in the race against Senator Patterson in 1934 he pledged full support to the New Deal.

Truman's political ideas also derived in part from his life in a small, farm-oriented town. Independence, with its courthouse and small businesses, churches, and schools, was the focal point of Jackson County. In this atmosphere, Truman absorbed the small-town ideal of looking to the main chance to strike it rich. His father, like many another citizen of Independence, was a speculator in land and livestock and eventually went broke. Harry Truman speculated in land, oil, mining, savings and loan associations, banking, and farming. He was continually "on the make" as small businessman, farmer, Mason, or National Guardsman. A small-town American, he shared the radical economic opinion so endemic in the Middle Border. He tended to see basic national economic questions in terms of conflict between individuals and the "interests" or corporations.

Finally, the experience which carried Harry Truman beyond the horizons of his small town was his service in France during World War I. For the first time, as commander of Battery D, 129th Field Artillery Regiment, he came into sustained contact with men outside the farm-town, lodge-brother, small-business dimension. Battery D, recruited mainly in the vicinity of Jesuit-operated Rockhurst College in Kansas City, consisted largely of Irish-Catholic college students and graduates. Prior to Truman's arrival as commander, Battery D had proved impossible to discipline, and three successive commanding officers had been relieved of command. Truman had been elected first lieutenant by his fellow members of Battery B before the unit was taken into federal service, and he represented the regiment's last alternative to breaking up Battery D, transferring all officers and men, and rebuilding with new personnel.

The new leader bluntly assumed command, demonstrating his innate strength of character and desire to succeed. He took personal charge of discipline in the battery, commanded it in four major engagements in France, enjoyed its hell-raising reputation, seldom resorted to a court-martial, and invariably addressed the troops in the vocabulary of a mule-skinner. Battery D's Irish-Catholic collegians brought out the true character and abilities of Harry Truman, Southern Baptist, Mason, small-town speculator. It was Battery D that transformed Truman from failure to success, from backwoods dabbler to clever politician. As Truman later said, "My whole political career is based upon my war service and war associates."

Truman did not overstate the case. Command taught him the value of organization as the best means of achieving an objective, and the challenge of organizing Battery D elicited from him the essentials of leadership. His command of Battery D was marked by an initial toughness which gave evidence of his competence, but he quickly developed an ability to put himself in the place of men accused of violating regulations. In Battery D he learned for the first time to project tolerance, personal concern, and loyalty outside his immediate family. His wartime experiences confirmed and invigorated incipient social impulses and political ambitions which had long lain unfocused in his character. Battery D directed Truman toward the presidency. Truman never forgot.

Observers familiar with Truman's record in Jackson County could have predicted his record in the Senate, and they might have foreseen the smooth transition he made from county affairs to national concerns, for national problems were not new to Senator Truman. From October 1933 until his nomination to the Senate in 1934 he had served as the unpaid Federal Reemployment Director for Missouri, working directly with Harry Hopkins. In January 1934, Truman told an audience at Columbia, Missouri: "We are now going about the job of redistributing wealth that was amassed in the robust years but, thank heaven, we are going about it more peacefully than was done in Russia, Germany, and Italy." This statement, made outside the context of a political campaign, may be regarded both as a refinement of the old populist teachings and as a preview of Truman's future economic attitudes as President of the United States.

TRUMAN AS UNITED STATES SENATOR

Within three months of taking the oath as United States senator, Truman was deeply involved in hearings before the Senate Committee on Interstate Commerce. Because the Democratic senator senior to Truman chose not to attend the hearings, it was Truman who conducted the investigation of civilian air commerce. He also wrote legislation, in collaboration with Republican Senator Warren Austin of Vermont, which passed into law as the Civil Aeronautics Act of 1938. In spite of heavy pressure from Missouri utility corporations against passage of the Utility Holding Act of 1935, Truman supported federal regulation of public utilities. During his service in the Senate Truman authored or coauthored the Truman-Hobbs Act of 1940, the Truck and Bus Amendment to the Interstate Commerce Act, and the Transportation Act of 1940, which still controls national transportation policy.

By 1938 Truman had gained a reputation as one of the most knowledgeable and hard-working members of the Senate, was respected for the quality and extent of his personal information, and was known as an expert on committee work. He had followed the New Deal lead in support of welfare measures, especially those designed to aid labor, farmers, the elderly, and the unemployed. Truman had also taken a strong liberal stand on reciprocal trade, regulation of industry and commerce, flood control, public power, civil liberties, and antilynching laws. His statements and votes on welfare legislation and civil rights marked him as an independent thinker who was often even more liberal than the Democratic leadership of the Senate.

Early in 1940, near the end of Truman's first term in the Senate, he was approached with the presidential proposal that he retire from the Senate in exchange for a seat on the Interstate Commerce Commission. An investigation of the Kansas City Democratic machine in 1938 had produced evidence which led to indictment of Tom Pendergast on charges of income tax evasion. In May 1939, Pendergast pleaded guilty to the charges and was sent to prison. Those in Washington, D.C., Franklin Roosevelt included, who thought of Truman as "Pendergast's office boy" were sure that the scandal had ended Truman's hopes for reelection in 1940. Roosevelt's message was simple. The President was sure that Truman could not gain reelection, and the New Deal would support another candidate in the coming primary. Truman's reply was characteristic: He would run if he got only a single vote—his own.

Truman fought a hard primary against both Roosevelt's candidate, Governor Lloyd C. Stark, and United States District Attorney Maurice Milligan, the man who had sent Tom Pendergast to jail and hoped to ride the anti-Pendergast tide to victory. At the Democratic National Convention of 1940, held in Chicago shortly before the Missouri primary, Governor Stark flaunted his White House support and made such an open bid to be nominated for the vice-presidency that many of his backers, including Robert C. Hannegan of Saint Louis, became embarrassed and withdrew their support. With the strong backing of Hannegan, labor, and the Negro vote, Truman triumphed in the three-man primary. And in November 1940, Truman won reelection to the Senate seat.

On August 22, 1940, even as Truman won political vindication, the sheriff of Jackson County foreclosed the Truman family farm. The mortgage represented money borrowed to repay the last of the haberdashery debts, but Senator Truman was financially unable to prevent the eviction of his mother and sister from the family land.

By the end of 1940, with France defeated and the Nazis at the English Channel, Congress had already appropriated over $25,000,000,000 for American defense preparations. Truman had had firsthand experience with the similar buildup for World War I, and, following his reelection, he took an automobile tour which led from Washington, D.C. to Florida, on to Texas, northward to Nebraska and Wisconsin, into Michigan, and back to Washington. On the trip he inspected army camps, defense plants, and military installations being built. He returned convinced that almost everywhere there was evidence of waste or potential for waste, growing out of both ignorance and outright fraud. On February 10, 1941, Truman proposed formation of the Senate Special Committee to Investigate the National Defense Program. As originator of the investigation, Truman was named chairman and began work on April 15, 1941. He remained active as chairman of the committee until he was nominated for the vice-presidency in August 1944.

The Truman Committee gained fame for its rigorous investigations, its hard but fair evaluations, its unwillingness to pull punches or shade analyses, and its refusal to play favorites with government, labor, or management. Truman, as chairman, accepted no evasions and insisted on following what eventually became the motto of the committee: "There is no substitute for a fact. When the facts are known, reasonable men do not disagree with respect to them."

The full impact of the Truman Committee on the war effort is incalculable in that it avoided duplication and promoted actual production. In essence, the committee brought order out of what was already becoming chaos early in 1941. It is generally agreed that the committee prevented some $15,000,000,000 of waste, while its very existence deterred would-be war profiteers. The success of the investigations, the direct result of Truman's administrative ability, brought the chairman increasingly into the view of Franklin Roosevelt and the American public. The Truman Committee remains today a model of productive congressional investigation, looking to solid achievement rather than widespread publicity for its members.

TRUMAN AS PRESIDENT

Roosevelt's successor was indeed no king. Neither was he the unknown incompetent too often described in accounts of the succession. Truman was Roosevelt's vice-presidential choice of a common man of uncommon character, ability, and training in public administration, and Truman proved the choice a wise one. Truman's first assessment of the presidential task, shortly following his assumption of the presidency, was made in the clear language of an experienced administrator: "Now it became my responsibility to lead— to recommend legislation, to administer the government, and to use the power and prestige of the presidency to induce sound social and political action." For Truman after Roosevelt's death, the presidency was a larger stage where larger powers could be used to assure the proper course of American progress.

As the war rushed toward its end in 1945, economic problems seemed of major importance to Truman, and he proposed to act. His action took the form of a message to Congress on September 6, 1945, a message at first obscured in the momentous events of the period: the surrender of Germany, the Potsdam Conference, the use of the world's first atomic bombs, and the fall of Japan. The President, as chief legislator, directed the attention of Congress to twenty-one specific areas of legislation and forwarded specific proposals. What he sought, although few were willing to read the clear language of his message, was a resolution of domestic policy which would set the course of the nation for at least a decade.

Franklin Roosevelt, in a final attempt to grapple with the promises and hazards of a postwar America, had included an "Economic Bill of Rights" in his 1944 State of the Union message. Striking out for the first time beyond his accustomed role of defender of, mediator for, and physician to capitalism and popular democracy, Roosevelt had couched his thoughts in typical philosophical language:

> *The right to a useful and remunerative job . . . The right to earn enough . . . The right of every farmer . . . The right of every businessman . . . The right of every family . . . The right to adequate medical care . . . The right of a good education . . . All these rights spell security.*

The declaration was inspirational but characteristically vague.

Truman's Fair Deal message of 1945 dutifully recited the Economic Bill of Rights but in addition proposed specific legislation and workable programs. In sum, Truman asked that Congress enact into law the essence of frontier radical thinking in regard to economics, society, and politics. But Truman did not regard his proposal as radical in any sense; instead he saw it as simply a program designed to bring about justice too long denied. It was to be the culmination of the long march of ideas from the Middle Border to the nation's capital; it was to be the crowning victory for the once-despised thinking of the Grangers, the Farmers' Alliances, the progressives, and the liberal movement. The Fair Deal went beyond progressivism and liberalism, because it proposed to harness permanently the American economy and political structure in pursuit of a specific goal: to improve the quality of life for all Americans. The Fair Deal was more than a defense of the capitalist mode of production and popularly controlled government; it was a forward-looking proposal, to be sustained with full presidential powers, to "make life more worthwhile" for all Americans.

The presidential cabinet which Truman inherited from Roosevelt was remarkably unsuited to the Fair Deal, both in temperament and outlook. In short order it gave way to men who shared Truman's analysis of national affairs. Except in the Department of State and in the new Department of Defense, Truman surrounded himself with men who recognized the old Middle Border enemies: the huge corporations, the houses of finance capital, the transportation monopolists, the agricultural middlemen, the predatory landlords and bankers, the utility manipulators, and those who enriched themselves by gouging the poor. The supplanting of the New Deal ameliorists by the Fair Deal radicals served as notice that Truman intended to embed the principles of frontier radicalism in the foundations of statutory law.

THE FAIR DEAL

The first Fair Deal message asked Congress to begin work immediately on specific measures: extension of social security and unemployment compensation; full employment legislation; a higher minimum wage; public and private housing programs; an employment service run solely by the federal government; strong farm price supports; public power systems for the Columbia, Arkansas, and Missouri rivers, as well as for the Central Valley of California; and a permanent Fair Employment Practices Commission to eliminate racial discrimination in employment. The President also promised to send up future messages on federal aid to education, expanded social security programs, and a national health plan. As a foundation for the Fair Deal, Truman asked Congress for new powers to reorganize the executive branch, a law to permit controlled reconversion of the national economy to peacetime production, and legislation to secure full employment to all persons wanting to work.

Truman obtained passage of the Reorganization Act of 1946, which permitted him to reorganize and reform the executive branch in accord with his own ideas and those generated by the study commission headed by former President Herbert Hoover. The result was to bring the executive branch under close presidential supervision and to increase White House abilities to direct the bureaucracy. He reformed the Internal Revenue Service to improve executive control, took personal charge of budget-making in conferences with the Director of the Budget, and obtained agreement from the Federal Reserve Board that the President would be sole money manager for the nation.

In accord with his views of operating the executive branch, Truman parceled out his various proposals among the cabinet and agency heads most concerned with them. The full-employment measure, however, was deemed to be of sufficient importance to be entrusted to the House majority leader, Congressman John W. McCormack of Massachusetts. McCormack, no frontier radical, supported the President and steered the bill to successful passage. The Employment Act of 1946, little understood at the time of its enactment, marks the watershed of American economic history in that it charges the federal government to use all its powers, coordinate all its plans, and employ all its resources to maintain conditions which would afford useful employment to all persons seeking to work. In short, the responsibility for insuring the nation's economic well-being was permanently transferred from the market to the President and Congress of the United States.

The Employment Act of 1946 required the congressional Joint Economic Committee (seven members of each house of Congress) to study and report to Congress on the state of the economy and programs to aid the national economy and to review the President's economic recommendations. It also created the Council of Economic Advisers, a three-man body, to provide expertise and advice regarding the national economy within the Executive Office of the President. Under the law, the President is required to furnish an economic report within sixty days of the opening of each session of the Congress which summarizes national economic conditions. The novel effect and major importance of the act of 1946 is that it substitutes politicians, elected by popular support, for the self-selected moguls of finance and captains of industry who had formerly guided the economy. The President became the actual director of the "managed economy" of the United States.

The act of 1946 was the only major portion of the Fair Deal enacted into law by the Seventy-ninth Congress before its expiration in January 1947. Both Congress and the President thus found themselves bedeviled by twin developments: the agonies of readjusting the economy to peacetime production and a flare-up of conflict with the Soviet Union. Both developments conspired to permit conservatives in both House and Senate to shirk the social responsibilities spelled out by the President in his first Fair Deal message, either calling themselves champions of "the American way of life" or stalwarts defending the nation against "godless, atheistic Communism." Not content with success in foiling the presidential demands for social justice and civil rights, they also took advantage of national war weariness to demand an end to all economic controls.

Not only conservatives impeded passage and implementation of Truman's Fair Deal. The wartime demands for patriotism and production for victory were sharply devalued by the approach of peace and a wave of labor-management disputes rolled across the nation in 1945 and early 1946. These disputes reached crisis proportions in the spring of 1946, when the President had to seize the coal mines to restore production and resort to a request to Congress that striking rail workers be drafted into the Army to prevent a national rail strike. By his decisive action Truman lost, at least temporarily, the political support of the labor unions. By their irresponsible actions the unions had effectively laid the foundation for punitive antiunion legislation, the Taft-Hartley Act of 1947.

THE COLD WAR: IMPEDIMENT TO THE FAIR DEAL

As Truman fought at home to convert the economy without paying the price of economic depression, foreign affairs demanded an ever-increasing portion of his time and effort. The Cold War, which began almost at the moment it was known that Hitler was dead, matched the United States and the Soviet Union in a blow-for-blow conflict. In retrospect, it is clear that the Cold War was based upon mutual misapprehensions of the contending superpowers. Stalin clearly expected that popular demand in the United

States to "bring the boys home" would require the rapid and total withdrawal of all American forces from Europe. The western reaches of the continent would then fall into the hands of indigenous Communist parties, and Soviet influence would reach the Atlantic by means of the ballot box.

Most Americans saw the Soviet Union in 1945 as a valiant ally, exhausted and devastated by German attack. Postwar Soviet policy would of necessity be devoted to rebuilding the Soviet Union rather than to plans for expansion of power. The initial economic aid given to Europe by the United States in the fall and winter of 1945–1946 was a simple humanitarian response to the devastation of Europe which had accompanied the reconquest of the continent. During that period there was almost no realization on the United States' part that such aid was perceived by the Soviet leaders as a counterattack on their policy. As late as February 1946, when Truman sat on the platform at Westminster College as Winston Churchill delivered his "Iron Curtain" speech, the ferocity of the clash of policy lay largely unforeseen.

By mid 1946, however, Truman had embarked on a definite course of action designed to prevent Soviet success in Europe. The spectacular collision of dissimilar political and economic systems cloaked the similarities of the opponents, making the conflict even more dangerous. Each was a missionary nation; each was secure in its own possession of the truth; each was zealous to export its system to the world. If the Soviets looked forward to a great Communist utopia, the United States saw a future global victory of popular democracy. Truman's European policy, founded upon the diplomatic brilliance of Dean Acheson and the military genius of George C. Marshall, eventually prevailed. The coup d'etat which felled Czechoslovakia's coalition government on February 25, 1948 provided the last European territorial gain for the Soviet bloc. After Czechoslovakia, Stalin's policy in western Europe was successfully contained, lost its dynamism, and ultimately failed.

A similar policy, combining economic aid and military alliances, was adopted in the Pacific following the fall of the Chinese Nationalists in 1949. What provided victory in China to Mao Tse-tung and the Chinese Communists probably had little to do with political ideology; rather it was the result of the inefficiency and corruption of the Chiang regime coupled with the general apathy of the Chinese people. Chiang's fall was important to the Fair Deal, however, since it permitted political paranoids in the United States to insist that Truman and Acheson had "lost China."

Concerning the underdeveloped nations, without apparent understanding of the nature of the "third world," United States aid went to the colonial powers to regain their possessions in Africa and Asia. Only in the cases of India and Israel did the United States recognize the general desire for independence by politically suppressed populations.

The great commotion caused by the Cold War provided a good excuse for Congress to refuse action on Truman's domestic policy. During the congressional elections of 1946, in a postwar backlash similar to that which swept Churchill from office in Britain in 1945, the voters entrusted control of both houses of Congress to the Republican party. Conservatives, openly pledged to undo the New Deal, assumed posts of leadership in both House and Senate, forming a complete and tireless opposition to the Fair Deal. The conservative coalition of northern Republicans and southern Democrats, which had allowed Roosevelt's wartime Fair Employment Practices Committee to die in 1946, firmly refused Truman's call to act on permanent civil rights legislation. The President's plans for aid to the elderly and the poor, for public housing, medical care, and public power were bottled up in committee or reached the legislative floor in such condition as to be worthless.

The same conservatives, however, effectively decontrolled prices, passed the Taft-Hartley Act, and enacted the National Security Act of 1947, which, though it diverged somewhat from Truman's recommendations, reorganized the nation's armed forces, strengthened presidential control over the armed forces, created the National Security Council to act as a presidential advisory board, and centralized under presidential control the gathering and evaluation of intelligence information. The act also gave legal sanction to the Joint Chiefs of Staff and directed them to report to the President on matters referred to them. The conservatives also provided enough votes to pass large military budgets, including financial aid to the Chinese Nationalist government. In their fear of Communism they even supported the Truman Doctrine of aid for Greece and Turkey and the Marshall Plan to rebuild the economy of Europe. Some liberal legislation, such as farm price supports and irrigation extension, was passed because the nature of the proposals split the ranks of conservatives.

By the end of 1947 Truman was clearly dissatisfied with the progress of the Fair Deal, and he determined to put Congress on notice that domestic programs held first priority and were the essential foundation for successful foreign policy. In his State of the Union message of January 1948, the President again thrust forward his demands that Congress act on his domestic program. The reason for the Fair Deal program, said Truman, was "the concern of an enlightened people that conditions [in America] be so arranged as to make life more worthwhile." Laying out his plan for the coming decade, the President declared that "year by year, beginning now, we must make substantial progress" toward this goal.

Truman stated his agenda in some detail: to secure fully the essential human rights of all American citizens; to protect and develop our human resources; to conserve and use the natural resources so they can contribute most effectively to the welfare of the people; to lift the standard of living for all Americans by strengthening our economic system and sharing more broadly among our people the goods we produce; and to achieve world peace based on principles of freedom, justice, and the equality of all nations. For each point of his national agenda, Truman proposed specific areas of attack and programs designed to achieve results. What Truman proposed in January 1948 was nothing less than a massive redistribution of the national wealth under direction of the President.

The message had purposes beyond fulfilling the legal requirement that the President report annually the state of the Union. It offered the occasion to restate the Fair Deal as the means of achieving the "good life" for all Americans within the decade. It also served as the opening salvo of the campaign of 1948. Truman's words were clearly directed to the public in an attempt to refocus popular attention toward needed domestic reforms and to displace the palpable fear of Communism already stalking the land in the persons of Chairman J. Parnell Thomas of the House Un-American Activities Committee, Congressman Richard Nixon of California, and Congressman Martin Dies of Texas.

THE ELECTION OF 1948

Truman determined to run for election in 1948 in the face of tremendous odds. Many Democrats saw Truman as doomed to defeat by a growing unpopularity, while liberal Democrats still longed for the dead monarch and viewed Truman as too conservative. Conservative Democrats understood too well the economic and social radicalism of the proposed Fair Deal, and other Democrats, anxious only to consolidate the party's hold on the White House, put forward the name of General Dwight D. Eisenhower. From Sam Rayburn they received the gruff reply, "Good man, but wrong job." Rayburn had the gift of prophecy.

Truman nominated himself in 1948 in recognition that his task as President was far from complete. He had just ended three years of dealing with a Congress dominated by conservatives, and he recognized their objective: Foil the Fair Deal, and dismantle the New Deal. The remedial and ameliorative measures of the New Deal had defended popular democracy and capitalism against both domestic and foreign foes. If the Fair Deal was to redirect America toward equality of political and economic life for all, it was essential that the Fair Deal become embedded in the foundations of statutory law. In short, the "national agenda" set by the Fair Deal messages of 1945 and 1948 demanded that Truman seek election.

The Democratic platform of 1948, except for a strengthened civil rights plank, was a restatement of the Fair Deal. Truman, in full control of the convention, arranged his own nomination and that of his running mate, Senator Alben Barkley of Kentucky. Henry Wallace's followers boycotted the convention in their haste to disassociate themselves from Truman's anti-Soviet policy, only to find themselves, for the most part, captives of Communist front organizations. The Dixiecrats, disguising their racism and fear of the Negro under the banner of "states' rights," fielded a ticket headed by Governor Strom Thurmond of South Carolina. Newspapers, magazines, and pollsters concluded that Truman was a defeated candidate, doomed by party disunity. In the entire nation, only two experienced politicians saw the President as a winner in 1948: Harry S Truman and Senator J. Howard McGrath of Rhode Island. McGrath was Truman's campaign manager.

Squabbling among the remaining Democrats at the convention delayed the President's acceptance speech until 2:00 A.M. on July 13, 1948, but the speech was worth waiting for. In his first sentence Harry Truman charged into the fray, swinging a political meat axe: "Senator Barkley and I will win this election and make those Republicans like it— Don't you forget that." The issue was simple, said the President: Either federal powers were to be used for the good of all Americans, or they were to be misused in the interests of special privilege. And that was the message hammered home by Harry Truman as he traveled by train almost 32,000 miles across America, delivering 356 speeches.

In every major city or country town the theme was the same: The voters could rally to him or allow conservatives and reactionaries to destroy the progress of the previous fifteen years. To emphasize his point, he called a special session of the Republican-dominated Eightieth Congress to meet before election day and demanded that it enact the liberal promises of the 1948 Republican platform. As Truman had foreseen, the "Turnip Day Session" of July 26, 1948 produced nothing. On that same day, however, the President signed Executive Order 9981, which declared the end to racial segregation in the nation's armed forces.

The story of the election of 1948 is well known. While Republican Thomas E. Dewey moved majestically from platitudinous peaks to Olympian pronouncements, Truman took his case to the voters. Everywhere he went the President waged a fighting campaign in which he lambasted his opponents with such a fine sense of aroused fury that he carried with him the "common men" who wanted to preserve both prosperity and reform. Other voters undoubtedly supported him as a peppery underdog who refused to surrender.

When election day was over, Truman had defeated Dewey by more than 2,000,000 votes, and he had put together a Fair Deal coalition.

Truman's Fair Deal coalition was new to Democratic party politics. Thurmond's candidacy had denied Truman four states of the "solid South," and the President had salvaged only Massachusetts and Rhode Island in the industrial Northeast. In New York, where Wallace's followers had mounted a major campaign, 500,000 Democratic votes had been siphoned off, to give the state to Dewey. Although Dewey was originally a small-town boy from Michigan before making his reputation in New York, he had little appeal in the farm states, except in Republican single-party enclaves in the Dakotas, Kansas, and Nebraska.

Truman's victory was fashioned largely to the west of the Ohio and Mississippi rivers, in the Midwest, the Southwest, and on the Pacific Coast, where the President took both California and Washington. It was in precisely those areas where frontier radical doctrines had been most readily accepted in earlier days that Truman won decisive victories. Almost without help, he had beaten back a massively financed Republican campaign, confounded the prognosticators, and vindicated his faith in popular democracy. Democrats also regained control of both houses of Congress, although the majority of twelve in the Senate and ninety-three in the House contained many enemies of the Fair Deal. Most important, Truman had won without support of the "lunatic left" or the reactionaries of the right.

TRUMAN'S SECOND TERM

Truman's 1949 State of the Union message reiterated his demands of 1945 and 1948 and, for the first time, made use of the term "Fair Deal" to describe the program. Even in victory, however, Truman's earlier exuberance was missing, an indication that he realized his congressional majorities were too slim. The inaugural address of 1949, delivered later in January, bears eloquent testimony that domestic reform and progress in America are too often the first victims of war. Speaking of a "decisive period" of challenge to the free world from the "false philosophy" of Communism, Truman laid out a plan by which democracy could be strengthened and world peace preserved. His four points—continued support for the United Nations, continued aid for world recovery, military help for free nations to forestall aggression, and the sharing of American agricultural and technological knowledge with underdeveloped nations—provide further evidence of Truman's clarity of policy judgment. But the Fair Deal had become a casualty of the Cold War; the entire inaugural address was devoted to foreign problems.

Some Fair Deal legislative gains were made by the President in cooperation with the Democratic Eighty-first Congress. The Housing Act of 1949 began an attack on city slums by funding 800,000 low-income housing units, and Congress amended the Fair Labor Standards Act in 1950 to raise the federal minimum wage to 75 cents per hour. The Farmers Home Administration, the Rural Electrification Administration, and the Tennessee Valley Authority received support previously denied by the Eightieth Congress. Further, the coverage of social security was broadened to include 10,000,000 additional individuals, and retirement benefit payments were increased. In a final Fair Deal gesture, Congress replaced the Immigration Act of 1948, which openly discriminated against Catholics and Jews, with the Displaced Persons Act of 1950, which allowed entry of 400,000 homeless Europeans in excess of the quotas.

By mid 1950 the new "Red scare" was building to a cacophony of wild charges. Fair Deal proposals for farm legislation, civil rights reform, federal aid to education, and federal health insurance failed of passage in Congress after massive campaigns had been mounted against them by special interests like the Farm Bureau Federation, the American Medical Association, and an *ad hoc* group of "professional Catholics." By June 24, 1950, when North Korean forces attacked South Korea, the Fair Deal legislative program was dead.

The year 1950 marked the nadir of the Fair Deal. Petty graft was discovered among White House aides and other federal officials; Secretary of State Dean Acheson, bound always by the code of the gentleman, refused to denounce his friend Alger Hiss in spite of Hiss's conviction of perjury; celebrated espionage trials resulted in the convictions of Soviet agents; and Truman made the unfortunate remark that attempts to ferret out security risks in his administration were a "red herring" designed to cloud the real issues. His statement was generally true but was subjected to savage misinterpretation. The 1950 elections gave the Republicans a gain of five seats in the Senate and twenty-eight in the House. From then on, the Fair Deal fought a purely defensive battle. All hope of working majorities in Congress was gone, and the attention of Americans was riveted on the war in Korea and on the rising fear of Communism at home and abroad. The combination of cold war and hot war caused a substitution of massive suspicion for rational analysis and planning; terror replaced reason.

EVALUATION OF TRUMAN'S PRESIDENCY

In private life Truman was a rather quiet person, moderate in his views, a trifle reserved in his dealings with others, and a man of deep and continuing interest in the well-being of his family, relatives, and friends. In almost every case of adversity which touched his personal circle, Truman was able to understand and forgive human frailties or simple bad luck. He was intensely loyal to his own, a trait which left him open to personal attack by his enemies.

As a public man, Truman was the political battler par excellence of his era. His joy at the prospect of a good political fight, particularly one which promised copious bloodshed, is legendary. As a national figure, however, Truman rose above parochialism and became a leader filled with optimism and courage. He chose to fight, against all comers, in promotion or defense of those ideals which seemed to him matters of principle. In any contest, domestic or international, Truman refused to flinch or blink away adverse events or information. His outstanding characteristics as President were his courage and will to prevail.

Truman's style was that of America's great midsection. He was unprepossessing in appearance but jovial in manner. His oratorical delivery was uninspiring, and his speeches claimed public attention only by virtue of his plain talk, clear reasoning, and unvarnished vocabulary. His willingness to operate openly and to explain fully how he reached decisions projected among his fellow citizens a real sense of participation in policy-making. Plain talk also produced broad popular support for Truman's policies, although on occasion it also served to create deep divisions of public opinion. The President saw no harm in that.

Truman had no fear of executive power as such, and the result was to free him of anxiety and hesitation in taking action. He perceived himself as the embodiment of the national will, and he wielded the awesome authority of the presidency, not for the aggrandizement of Harry S Truman, but simply as the citizen selected by the nation to perform the duties of the office. As President, Truman retained his lifelong faith in popular democracy and the efficacy of the ballot box in selecting those who shall govern. His sole concern was "the responsibility that I felt to the people who had given me this power."

His vital sense of presidential responsibility grew out of his definition of the presidential task: to work in the interest of the people. "In order to do that the President must use whatever power the Constitution does not expressly deny him." The institution was plastic to his will. His expansive view of the presidency brought him to question the effectiveness of the office in terms of the ultimate goal of the nation. Long before he entered the White House, Truman had determined the all-encompassing goal of the American nation and its government to be the perfection of the quality of American life by full and wise use of its human, social, and natural resources. He resolved to create, in the presidency, an instrument appropriate to carrying out the great national task.

The contemporary American presidency rests upon a triad of legislation obtained by Truman immediately after World War II: the Executive Reorganization Act of 1946, the Employment Act of 1946, and the National Security Act of 1947. Taken in concert, the result of these laws is to grant the President effective control and direction of the federal bureaucracy, the national economy, and the military forces of the United States. Coupled with the almost untrammeled competences in foreign policy conferred on the President by the Constitution, the laws of 1946 and 1947 created the contemporary presidential authority. Thus the President became the sole national policy-maker while Congress evolved into a legislative body which reacts to the presidential initiative.

Truman's reform of the presidential institution stands in stark contrast to earlier agglomerations of power in the presidency. Although much of Truman's increases of executive competence went unappreciated at the time (especially the economic implications of the Employment Act of 1946), the office was being shaped as a tool adequate to presidential tasks. Truman was the architect of what we accept today as the contemporary presidency. Following Truman's reformation and reconstruction of the presidency, it is more proper to speak of presidential authority than to single out and dismiss executive actions as mere exercises of power. Through consciously pursued reform of the presidency, Truman placed the contemporary President at the pinnacle of authority and responsibility in an office equipped to meet every challenge and to move, for well or for ill, to achieve the national goal.

In contradiction of his organizational abilities, Truman tended toward administrative inflexibility. His experience and preference led him to depend upon his cabinet for advice and information, although he pointedly reserved all decisions for himself. He entrusted major legislation to the care of the executive department heads, often with less than excellent results. In spite of his ten years of service in the Senate, Truman maintained no permanent liaison with Congress, and he undoubtedly paid the price of lack of current information regarding congressional trends. His legislative leadership of Congress was intermittent, as he moved to promote or defeat specific legislation, and his almost unprecedented use of the presidential veto and the executive order bear testimony to his inability to lead commanding majorities in the Congress.

In direct contrast to his rigid administrative stance, Truman's flexibility and decisiveness provided the motive power to the contemporary presidency. He proved keenly perceptive of the demands of policy, and his rational approach to problems permitted him to arrive at major determinations which seldom required revision, even when those decisions demanded drastic changes in national outlook. Truman's policy stances on use of the atomic bomb, aid to Greece and Turkey, the Berlin airlift, the defense of South Korea, and even aid to Communist Yugoslavia remain unquestioned today except by revisionist historians who fail to understand the enormity of the alternatives.

Truman was indeed a radical. He was radical in that he conceived a presidential authority limited only by express prohibitions of the Constitution, a foreign policy designed to reshape the structure of the world's diplomatic and economic systems, and a series of programs by which the national wealth of the United States would be redistributed. In reorganizing the presidency Truman succeeded in forging the tool which, properly employed, permits the nation to deal with unprecedented and unforeseen crises at home and abroad. In reshaping the world's diplomatic and economic structures, his policy has endured for almost a generation. In his fight to redistribute the national wealth, Truman fell victim to the unremitting pressures of necessary foreign policy decisions as well as his own lack of effective leadership of Congress.

In terms of bringing about final passage of his domestic legislative program, Truman must be adjudged a failure. Most of his successes with Congress, except for the foundation stones of the Fair Deal, which have been discussed, were mere extensions of the New Deal. Yet he succeeded, in his Fair Deal messages of 1945, 1948, and 1949, in formulating the permanent national agenda. He prevailed because he impressed upon the political conscience of America his concern that "conditions be so arranged as to make life more worthwhile" for all Americans. In creating the contemporary presidency, in engraving in the bedrock of statutory law the radical frontier concept of redistributing the national wealth, and in setting the permanent national agenda, Truman raised a standard against which each of his successors must be judged.

NOTES

Pre-Presidential Years: The most detailed account of Truman's early life and entry into politics is in Jonathan Daniels, *The Man of Independence* (1950), pp. 1–156. Cabell Phillips, in his book *The Truman Presidency* (1966), handles the same period more concisely and with less sympathy.

Truman's Thought Processes: Truman's clarity of analysis and methods of decision-making are best summarized in Dean Acheson, *Present at the Creation* (1969), pp. 730–733.

Presidential Rhetoric: Truman, in his *Memoirs by Harry S Truman* (1955, 1956, two volumes), set the rhetoric within which his presidency must be discussed. The openness of approach and avoidance of hindsight more than make up for occasional minor errors of fact or obviously opinionated reporting.

Truman's Analysis of National Problems: Truman's close ties with Senator Burton K. Wheeler of Montana, who reinforced Truman's faith in the old populist and Bryan political philosophies, and with Justice Louis D. Brandeis, an unswerving enemy of monopoly and economic concentration of power, form a major foundation of the President's analysis of national problems. Together they helped Truman to articulate ideas regarding a more equal distribution of the national abundance which took the form of the Fair Deal.

Economic Power: Herbert Stein, *The Revolution in Fiscal Policy* (1969), Chapter 9, holds that the transfer of power to direct the national economy from private leaders to the President was an act of national consensus, although Stein notes the sharp debate in Congress and the general lack of public understanding of the importance of the Employment Act of 1946. Stein is currently chairman of the Council of

Economic Advisers in the Nixon administration. The best study of the council is by E. S. Flash, Jr., *Economic Advice and Presidential Leadership* (1969).

Truman vs. Labor: Truman's difficulties with labor are vividly sketched in his *Memoirs,* vol. 2, pp. 498–505.

The Cold War: The Cold War has been often described and much debated. Those who insist upon interpreting the clash as conscious policy on the parts of the superpowers reckon without the three great realities of 1945–1947: the general war weariness in both the U.S. and U.S.S.R.; the preponderance of Soviet ground forces on the European continent; and the American monopoly of the atom bomb. Those realities foreclosed any possibility of "military victory" for either side and provided overwhelming evidence that neither side planned the Cold War.

1948 Fair Deal Message: The text of this message is in the New York *Times,* January 8, 1948.

1948 Campaign: Truman's account of the campaign of 1948 is in his *Memoirs,* vol. 2, Chapter 15.

Frontier Radicalism: The clearest and best reasoned statement of frontier radicalism to be printed in the 1930s, following attempts by major corporations to suppress the work, is W. P. Webb, *Divided We Stand* (1937), pp. 168–176. Truman's most cogent summary of Middle Border radicalism came in his speech in Saint Louis in 1948, printed in John A. Garraty and Robert A. Devine, *Twentieth Century America* (1968), pp. 520–526.

Two Views of Truman: Dean Acheson, in *Present at the Creation,* p. 729, sees Truman as one of the great Presidents by virtue of his leadership, his rational approach to problems, and his capacity for firm decisions. A revealing portrait of Truman is in Margaret Truman, *Harry S. Truman* (1973).

3. *Dwight D. Eisenhower: Mandate for Change*

In the fall of 1951, as national bewilderment and frustration continued to mount under the pressures of Korean combat and under charges of Communists in high places and corruption in the Truman administration, Senator Henry Cabot Lodge, Jr., visited the NATO commander in Paris. There Lodge told General Eisenhower that the purpose of his mission was to save the United States from a steady accumulation of power in Washington, D.C., increased paternalism in government dealings with citizens, endless deficit spending, and a constant erosion of the value of the dollar. Lodge pointed out to Eisenhower, with some emotion, that no Republican had held the presidency in twenty years and that the nation could avoid imminent danger only if corrective measures were taken by a Republican administration.

The years following 1932 had seen the Democrats emerge as the majority party. In five successive elections the Republican party had engaged the Democrats, and five times it had gone down to defeat. To Lodge the reason was certain and simple: The Republicans had taken on the appearance of people dedicated only to opposition. Lodge's candor was refreshing. He maintained that the Old Guard was out of touch with reality; that if Taft should gain the nomination, he would be defeated; that even Lodge himself could not win. For the Republicans to win in 1952 the presidential candidate must be a national hero who could attract independents and dissident Democrats without dividing the faction-riven Republican party. Considerations of practical politics made Eisenhower the ideal Republican candidate; he could register as a party member at a later date.

Lodge's words, while they did not immediately persuade Eisenhower to seek the presidency, did excite his thoughts. Early in 1948, on the occasion of his inauguration as president of Columbia University, Eisenhower had also denounced paternalism, which could suffocate the "will of a people to maintain a high degree of individual responsibility."

While Eisenhower pondered, leading Republicans acted. On February 10, 1952, aviatrix Jacqueline Cochran appeared at Eisenhower's quarters with a film of a "Draft Eisenhower" rally held in Madison Square Garden two days earlier. The general was understandably impressed by the enthusiastic support from a crowd of 15,000. Less than a week later, General Lucius Clay, in Britain for the funeral of George VI, invited Eisenhower to meet with two old friends, George Allen and Sid Richardson. At the meeting Eisenhower was persuaded to wind up his NATO business, return to the United States, and seek the presidency as a Republican.

Eisenhower's conception of his role in the election of 1952 diverged sharply from that perceived by Lodge and the liberal Republican leaders, who were primarily interested in electing a Republican President. Eisenhower concluded that he must respond to the call of duty, that he should go home and accept the burden of saving the nation. General Clay had already assured election officials in New Hampshire that Eisenhower was a Republican, and his victories in the New Hampshire and Minnesota primaries had had serious repercussions for the candidacy of Senator Robert A. Taft of Ohio. Assured of a viable campaign effort for nomination and convinced that America needed him, Eisenhower wrote to President Truman and requested to be relieved of all

NATO duties on June 1, 1952. As he turned homeward, he felt the keen sense of uncertainty which had affected George Washington's decision to accept the presidency.

By the time Eisenhower reached home in the summer of 1952, he had already determined to lead a "crusade for freedom" in the United States and abroad. An apocalyptic vision of the great clash of opposing forces of darkness and light was the constant theme of Eisenhower's search for delegates and his campaign against Democrat Adlai E. Stevenson. Throughout, Eisenhower stood on the high ground of morality and refused to engage in the general clamor of "the politicians." So clear was his sense of political morality that he was able to pierce even the murky waters of Texas politics to recognize the legitimacy of the Eisenhower delegates in their fight against the Taft men of Texas.

MILITARY CAREER OF
DWIGHT D. EISENHOWER

Despite his own words, Eisenhower was no "political novice." He had not engaged in partisan politics as had MacArthur and Clay, but his military record disclosed his possession of no mean political talent and ability to work within a system which is often more devious and perilous than partisan politics. He, a farm boy from Abilene, had been graduated by the United States Military Academy in a respectable position in the class of 1915. He obtained command of a military training facility in World War I, and he moved on to become military aide to the Assistant Secretary of War. He attended the Staff and Command School and was assigned as aide to General Douglas MacArthur during MacArthur's term as Army Chief of Staff. Following MacArthur's retirement from the Army and his appointment to command the Philippine Scouts, Eisenhower was sent to

Manila as senior adviser to MacArthur. In 1939 Eisenhower returned to the United States to plan the first large military maneuvers of the Army before World War II.

As plans for the Anglo-American invasion of North Africa took shape in 1942, Eisenhower was selected by General George C. Marshall to command the American forces. From command in Africa, Eisenhower successfully moved to the post of Supreme Commander of Allied Forces in Europe and eventually became Army Chief of Staff. After a few years in civilian life and following the signing of the NATO treaties, President Truman recalled Eisenhower to active duty and appointed him to the command of all NATO forces. The farm boy had done well in uniform; he had achieved every post of military prestige and power within the gift of the United States and its European allies.

Eisenhower's success in "getting along" with people became legendary during World War II. He dealt directly with Roosevelt, Churchill, de Gaulle, and various Soviet officials regarding the conduct of the war. He presided over a headquarters at London which successfully blended such disparate elements as the Free French, British, Australians, Greeks, Americans, Canadians, and Israeli officers serving with the British. From London he also commanded the invasion of Normandy, the reduction of Fortress Europa, and the manners and deportment of both Field Marshal Sir Bernard Law Montgomery and Lieutenant General George S. Patton. Eisenhower brooked no dissension among his staff or any incident which might imperil the success of his "crusade in Europe."

THE ELECTION OF 1952

Throughout the fight for delegates and the campaign for the presidency in 1952, the Eisenhower style and rhetoric remained constant. In his acceptance speech to the cheering Republican convention he accepted the summons "to lead a crusade for freedom in America and freedom in the world." His campaign laid great emphasis on the pre-Truman problems of the balanced budget, integrity in government, agricultural price supports, and formal diplomatic representation for the United States at the Holy See. He promised to restore the nation to a high moral position, to halt the work of subversives, to rebuild the old individualism, and to end the war in Korea. The campaign was an old-style drive to capitalize on discontent, disillusionment, and disappointment. Americans had fought a harsh war and displayed unprecedented generosity to their former enemies and friends, but the future still looked bleak. Eisenhower spoke in generalities, offended no one, and achieved the presidency.

Eisenhower's Democratic opponent, the relatively unknown Governor of Illinois, was selected by President Truman and gained nomination on the third ballot of the convention. Adlai E. Stevenson had made his mark in international affairs before demonstrating exceptional administrative ability in the governorship of his native state. During World War II and immediately after its close, he had headed important economic missions, and he had participated in both the San Francisco Conference of 1945 and the organizational meeting of the United Nations Assembly as special assistant to the Secretary of State. Stevenson was an intellectual whose incisive mind and capacity for penetrating analysis excited great respect and loyalty among those who knew him well. His fatal political flaw was an unwillingness to oversimplify issues in order to assume a more popular stance. His speeches were well reasoned and approached the nation's problems with clarity and precision, escaping oppressiveness only through the humor which was so much a part of the man. Running against a popular hero, heading a party whose southern wing had openly defected, and fighting the Republican cry, "It's time for a change," Stevenson was never a real contender in 1952. And his popular appeal had not improved any by the time he ran again in 1956, only to lose to Dwight Eisenhower by a larger margin.

Eisenhower carried all but nine states in 1952, although Stevenson gathered more votes than Truman polled in 1948. Large numbers of new voters and party switchers combined with all wings of the Republican party to give Eisenhower a plurality of almost 6,500,000 votes over his rival. In the "solid South" Eisenhower carried Virginia, Florida, Louisiana, and Texas. Stevenson won only eighty-nine votes; Eisenhower immediately interpreted his mandate. The President-elect believed he had been called to lead the new crusade against paternalism and the "creeping socialism" which he and Senator Taft had agreed was a major threat to America. The general theme with which the new administration began to plan its programs was based on the conscious intention to rid the nation of the New Deal and the Fair Deal, to grub out, root and branch, the twenty years of paternalism under Roosevelt and Truman. The illusion that such was the mandate of the voters was strengthened by the support for Eisenhower of die-hard conservatives in the South—Richardson, Shivers, and Daniel in Texas, plus James Byrnes of South Carolina. Senator Harry Byrd of Virginia contributed his benevolent neutrality to the last successful rally of the Dixiecrats and the "old Right" of the Republican party.

THE CABINET AND WHITE HOUSE STAFF

The Eisenhower cabinet was strongly conservative. Leading the cabinet as Secretary of State was John Foster

Dulles, a corporation lawyer of long international experience and a believer in strong action against Communist nations. Charles E. Wilson, former head of General Motors, became Secretary of Defense, while George M. Humphrey, former chairman of the Marcus A. Hanna Company of investment bankers, was named Secretary of the Treasury. Ezra Taft Benson, a member of the Council of Twelve of the Mormon Church and an avowed enemy of farm price supports, was appointed Secretary of Agriculture. Selected as Secretary of Commerce was Sinclair Weeks, a Massachusetts manufacturer long associated with the United States Chamber of Commerce. The cabinet contained no member of the academic community but included one Democrat as Secretary of Labor, Martin Durkin of the Plumbers Union. (As one quipster put it—nine millionaires and a plumber!) It was a cabinet consciously created by the new President to dismantle and destroy the New Deal and the Fair Deal. Eisenhower had no intention to move forward the Truman agenda; instead he proposed to eliminate it.

The inaugural address carried forward the apocalyptic tone which had marked the campaign of 1952, referring to the "forces of good and evil" massed and opposed as seldom before in history. The State of the Union message reminded the people of the grim fact of confrontation of the United States by Communist forces around the globe and called for the free nations to unite in self-defense. And Eisenhower had decided that his domestic policy would not be a continuation of the New Deal and Fair Deal. The President announced that he would seek efficiency in defense, reduce the federal deficits, balance the budget, check inflation, and free "the forces of private economic initiative." He also promised to rid the federal establishment of security risks and reorganize the structure of government in the interest of efficiency. As evidence that the policies of the nation had changed, the President announced that he would begin steps to eliminate economic controls "in an orderly manner." By his own estimate, the President's proposals were "revolutionary activity."

Inside the White House the new President was engaged in a major reorganization of the staff. Truman had operated the staff of the Executive Office of the President and his personal assistants with little regard for formal organization. As we have seen, the Truman congressional liaison was a sometimes thing, and tasks regarding the executive himself were parceled out on the basis of the ability or availability of a particular staff member.

Eisenhower's education and career experiences had convinced him of the value of organization, and he determined to fix both powers and responsibilities of the White House personnel. For his permanent congressional liaison he chose an old friend whose years of representing the Army on Capitol Hill had made him an intimate of many congressmen, Major General Wilton B. Persons. To aid Persons, Gerald D. Morgan and Bryce N. Harlow were named. Both had served with major committees of Congress, Morgan in drafting the Taft-Hartley Act and Harlow as staff director of the House Armed Services Committee. To deal with the press, the President appointed James C. Hagerty, who had been an active journalist before serving Thomas E. Dewey as press secretary.

Eisenhower also chose to organize the various presidential advisers in terms of echelon and responsibility. As the Assistant to the President, Eisenhower named former Governor Sherman Adams of New Hampshire, an early supporter and a leader in the floor fight against the Taft delegates at the convention. All matters taken up with the President and all papers read by the President required Adams' knowledge and approval. The Eisenhower staff was closely structured; it had its organization charts, its routing slips, its stamps and arrows, and its different colors of paper indicating who had originated a project or question. Although the White House staff organization was ridiculed by Eisenhower's political enemies and decried as rampant militarism, it was a system with which Eisenhower had dealt throughout his adult life.

Sherman Adams was not, however, Assistant President of the United States. Adams's power was considerable, but the true assistant to Eisenhower, as the President wished, was Vice-President Richard M. Nixon. From the start of the Eisenhower administration the Vice-President was treated as an executive officer rather than as a legislative official available mainly to replace a dead President. As Eisenhower's executive officer, Nixon sat in on all meetings of the cabinet, and he was officially appointed to the National Security Council. The importance of Eisenhower's innovation in the role of Vice-President became of great importance during Eisenhower's illnesses, when Nixon presided over cabinet meetings and sessions of the National Security Council.

In addition to altering the organization of the White House staff and the role of the Vice-President, Eisenhower changed the National Security Council to suit his needs. The council was created by the National Security Act of 1947 and consisted under Truman of the Secretary of Defense; the heads of the State Department, the Army, the Navy, and the Air Force; and the chiefs of the Munitions Board, the Research and Development Board, and the National Security Resources Board. The President headed the National Security Council, which served him as an advisory agency. At the urging of President Truman, the National Security Act of 1949 was passed and, among other more important military changes, eliminated the presence of the Secretaries of the Army, Navy, and Air Force from the council. Yet the council remained an unwieldy body, and Truman preferred to consult with the chairman of the Joint Chiefs of Staff on military matters.

Unlike Truman, whose major faith in the military was based on the familiar Missouri twang of General Omar N. Bradley, Eisenhower saw the National Security Council as a sort of "war cabinet," and he determined to strengthen it. Not only did the Vice-President become a member of the council, but the Secretary of the Treasury was also in attendance. The President also created two additional staff agencies for the council: the Planning Board and the Operations Coordinating Board. Both boards functioned continuously, keeping in close contact with the new Secretariat of the Council. Through such means the President hoped to be ready for every contingency.

Out of the changes in the White House staff and the National Security Council came the kind of "completed staff work" with which Eisenhower was so comfortable. Both the White House staff and the National Security Council provided the President with certain "preferred actions" or "best alternatives" to questions or problems which required presidential decisions. Eisenhower was, however, not a captive of either of his advisory agencies. Although he did not possess the benefit of a university education, Eisenhower was highly intelligent and deeply committed to carrying out his responsibilities. He preferred the staff method which provided him with "best alternatives," but he made his own decisions, as proper for the chief executive of the nation. His innate balance in and recognition of his position was forcefully demonstrated during the battle of Dien Bien Phu, when he rejected the advice of military and civilian advisers alike to employ American air power and possibly ground forces to rescue the French position in Vietnam.

The charge that Eisenhower was isolated from national problems and questions requiring presidential initiatives is, of course, nonsense. His staff system, often seen as the instrument of his supposed isolation, was his own creation, and he designed it to prevent the referral of all questions to the White House. He firmly believed in delegated authority, and he intended that the heads of administrative departments and agencies would run their agencies under his general directives. In addition, he believed that he had been elected to reduce the powers of the central government and the overwhelming dominance of the central government by the President, and that his staff system was one step in that direction.

EISENHOWER'S LEGISLATIVE PROGRAM

Eisenhower lost no time in supplying his list of legislative projects to Congress. Early in February 1953, he called for the admission of Hawaii as a state, legislation to transfer title to the states of oil-bearing federal land beyond the national territorial waters, an amendment to Taft-Hartley to eliminate patently unfair provisions, extension of the reciprocal trade agreements, and addition of two members to the Board of Commissioners of the District of Columbia. These measures the President found in consonance with his goals: to encourage "free men to trade competitively; to confirm the rights and responsibilities of the states; to give labor and management a square deal, with no coddling, no favoritism, no coercion."

The new President was interested in more than the legislative process. Late in April he announced his new doctrine of "massive retaliation" as the foundation of the defense policy, adding that the Secretary of the Treasury would join the National Security Council and that all future NSC policy papers were to include the cost of any proposed action. Reorganization Plan Number One, effective March 12, 1953, created the Department of Health, Education, and Welfare. Mrs. Oveta Culp Hobby, wartime head of the Women's Army Corps, became Secretary. On July 10, the President approved an act creating the second Hoover Commission to recommend economy in government, and he also created the Commission on Intergovernmental Relations. The latter commission was formed to investigate the division of responsibilities among federal, state, and local governments and scrutinize in detail all federally funded programs of aid to state or local governments. To head the commission Eisenhower appointed Clarence Manion, whose ultraconservative views were well known through the Manion Forum broadcasts.

The number and variety of changes within the executive branch revealed the President to be a man of outstanding organizational ability, ready to move toward his goals of smaller government, more efficient government, and cheaper government. To help him in his task he had recruited men of the Right for the cabinet, for subcabinet posts, for legislative liaison, and for the new commissions on efficiency. Eisenhower's actions during the first few months of his administration made clear his determination to carry out his mandate to dismantle and destroy the New Deal and Fair Deal.

The voters had chosen to give overwhelming support to the Republican presidential candidate in 1952, but they had done otherwise with Republican congressional candidates. When the Eighty-third Congress organized in 1953, Republicans controlled the Senate only through Wayne Morse's decision to vote with his old party, Morse having declared himself an independent. In the House the Republican majority stood at eleven members only. Worse, leading

Republican congressmen had long operated as snipers in opposition to progressive measures, and their support of the administration could be assured only by reactionary proposals. Eisenhower himself, convinced that the power of the presidency had grown too great, tended to defer to Congress as representative of the people. He had neither the inclination nor the votes to bind the Congress.

Robert A. Taft, the Majority Leader who had been spurned by the 1952 Republican convention as too conservative, appeared a flaming liberal beside Republican Senators Dworshak and Welker of Idaho, Butler of Nebraska, Malone of Nevada, Jenner of Indiana, and McCarthy of Wisconsin. Senator John Bricker of Ohio, Dewey's running mate in 1944, led the Senate Judiciary Committee. Senator William A. Knowland of California, chairman of the Republican Policy Committee, shared the leadership of the Committee of One Million with Congressman Walter Judd of Minnesota. (The Committee of One Million was commonly known as "the China lobby," and Knowland was derided as "the Senator from Formosa.") Henry Cabot Lodge, Jr., was not present when the Senate reconvened in 1953, having been defeated by Congressman John F. Kennedy of Massachusetts.

Even without the snipers the work of Persons and Harlow was difficult. The leaders of both houses were basically men of the Right. Taft was Senate Majority Leader; Joseph W. Martin had been elected Speaker of the House. Senator Eugene Milliken headed the Senate Finance Committee, with Congressman Dan Reed as chairman of the House Ways and Means Committee. The House Majority Leader was Charles Halleck; and Leslie Arends served as House Whip. Of the entire congressional leadership only Senate Majority Whip Leverett Saltonstall and Styles Bridges, chairman of the Senate Appropriations Committee, could be considered moderates. Most important to Eisenhower's legislative program, the Republican leaders were committed to curbing executive power by any and all means: administration proposals had riders attached; some were bottled up in committee; resolutions challenging the President's foreign policy were introduced; the Bricker Amendment to the Constitution, which would nullify presidential power to conduct foreign policy, was barely defeated in the Senate; and confirmation of key diplomatic appointees was assured only by solid Democratic support.

When the Eighty-third Congress ended in 1955, Eisenhower congratulated himself on five accomplishments in the first two years of his incumbency: he had successfully led the economic conversion from the Korean War to peacetime without depression; he had established a partnership with the electric power industry which would multiply generating facilities in the nation; he had checked profligate spending and restored fiscal responsibility in government; he had sponsored massive construction projects including the Saint Lawrence Seaway; and he had brought peace to the Republican party. With luck and considerable support from Democrats, he had withstood the assault by reactionary Republicans.

In the congressional elections of 1954 the President's party lost control of both houses of Congress. The Democrats gained a single-vote margin in the Senate and a more comfortable twenty-nine vote majority in the House. Even as the Democrats were on their way to restoring their "normal" control of Congress, Eisenhower was rethinking his mandate for change. In the summer of 1954, during the abortive second session of the Eighty-third Congress and the McCarthy uproar, the President defined his philosophy of government in a letter to an old friend. Gone were the decisions to dismantle the New Deal and the Fair Deal; there was no talk of "revolutionary activity" to reverse the trends of twenty years; even the term "paternalism" had faded away. In their place was the "middle way," which rejected federal control of every facet of individual life as well as dreams of achieving laissez-faire by doing away with every federal program representing "social advance." But Eisenhower would not hesitate to use federal powers to combat "cataclysmic economic disasters which can, in some instances, be even more terrible than convulsions of nature."

From the actions of the early Eisenhower administration as well as the President's personal account of those years it appears that he believed he had been called to defend freedom by ending paternalism, which he equated with the New Deal and Fair Deal. During his first two years in office Eisenhower sought major change, both in direction and content of national policy, and he abandoned Truman's agenda for social, political, and economic action. In civil rights he stated that sufficient legislation had already been passed and that further gains could be made through enforcement. In place of Truman's call for a national program to extend basic medical care for all citizens, Eisenhower recommended a limited measure to encourage private health insurance plans. In public housing Eisenhower asked that only 140,000 units be built in a four-year period.

EISENHOWER'S FOREIGN POLICY

Eisenhower's first two years as President were prophetic of his later interest in foreign policy. A major charge of Republican campaigners in 1952 had been that the Truman administration was not "tough" on the Communist enemies. In particular Truman was charged with having lost China, acquiescing in Soviet control over eastern Europe, and failing to defeat the Communists in Korea. Eisenhower moved quickly to change the Truman policies. In February 1953, the new administration unofficially notified the Chinese and North Koreans of its willingness to use all weapons, including nuclear devices, unless attacks on United Nations' troops ceased and the Koreans came to an armistice. The Chinese were told that the United States no longer felt constrained to limit combat to the Korean peninsula.

On balance, the Eisenhower foreign policy engaged in greater bombast and confrontation than that of Truman. Secretary of State John Foster Dulles proposed to honor the campaign promise to liberate the "captive nations" of eastern Europe, but no explanation of how this could be accomplished short of war with the Soviets was ever offered. In the 1953 State of the Union message, the President announced that the Seventh Fleet, stationed in the Strait of Formosa, would no longer shield the coasts of Communist China from assault by the Nationalists. As the Committee of One Million saw it, Chiang had been "unleashed" to attack Red China. The chief objector to the "unleashing" was Chiang himself, and by December 1954 the administration had signed the Formosa Defense Pact, under which Chiang agreed to avoid attacks on the mainland. In February 1955, American naval units evacuated Nationalist troops from the Tachen Islands off the coast of China, and the Truman Order of June 27, 1950, which required the Seventh Fleet to prevent a Communist attack on Formosa, was reinstated.

Eisenhower also made a rapid shift away from Truman's use of conventional forces to contain Soviet and Chinese expansion. The new military doctrine of massive retaliation relied upon bombers equipped with nuclear weapons to deter aggression by the Soviet Union or the Chinese Communists. The new policy had a threefold attraction: it employed advanced technology to replace ground forces; it took advantage of American nuclear superiority; and it saved money. The military budget of 1955 cut Army funds by over $4,000,000,000, and naval expenditures were reduced by $500,000,000 from 1954. The Air Force budget rose by some $800,000,000 to accommodate the new policy. The doctrine of massive retaliation became a hallmark of the Eisenhower years, and Eisenhower's adoption of the new policy resulted in grumbling by the Joint Chiefs of Staff, the inelegant assessment of the doctrine as "a bigger bang for a buck," and a campaign issue in the election of 1960.

SHIFTS IN DOMESTIC AND FOREIGN POLICY

The years 1953 and 1954 saw change in the Eisenhower drive toward the Right in domestic affairs and his belligerent stance in foreign affairs. Although the President continued to insist that his "mandate for change" remained constant, he began to redefine the limits and thrust of the mandate of 1952. In electing Eisenhower, the voters were clearly worried about Korea, Communism, and corruption as threats to the nation. The results in 1952 were a clear indication that the voters wanted an end to the Korean War, that they perceived a need for more telling action against Communism, and that they feared there was corruption in the Truman administration. The voters failed to see any threat to freedom in what the Democrats had been doing, and they had issued no mandate to wipe out the social gains of the previous twenty years. There had been no need for a "crusade"; Eisenhower had simply misunderstood his mandate in the welter of campaign rhetoric.

Eisenhower learned of his error in short order, since there was a plentitude of instructors—the entrenched conservatives of his own party and those among the Democrats. These forces put him under almost instant attack when they discovered that his conservatism lacked the visceral hatred which characterized their own opposition to Roosevelt and Truman. When Eisenhower sought to reduce the expenditures for armaments, he faced constant sniping from the military lobby and endless attempts by the congressional committees to enlarge the amount he requested. He asked for a three-year extension of the Trade Agreements Act and ran into a thicket of protectionists from both parties. He had to settle for a one-year continuation. Eisenhower's requests for increases in postal rates to make the postal service more nearly self-supporting were drowned in a sea of opposition until 1958, when Congress raised the rates and voted salary increases for postal workers, which consumed almost half of the increased postal income. Congress inevitably cut his budget requests, and Congressman Dan Reed, chairman of the House Ways and Means Committee, incessantly tried to cut taxes as a means of forcing the administration to reduce expenditures below the minimum needs of the federal agencies. Whereas Franklin Roosevelt as President was a teacher to the nation, Dwight David Eisenhower developed into an avid student of Congress, its moods and its intransigence.

Eisenhower found himself, during his first two years in office, constantly outflanked by the forces of the Right in both parties. Domestic Communism and the threat of revolution were the consistent themes of Republicans Mundt and Jenner, while the ultimate attack on Communists in government and the Army, including the charge that Eisenhower himself was soft on the conspirators, came from Republican Senator Joseph R. McCarthy. Ezra Taft Benson, Secretary of Agriculture, unceasingly preached free agricultural markets and the end of price supports, keeping farmers in an increasing state of anxiety. John Foster Dulles constantly reminded both Soviets and Europeans of Eisenhower's promise to liberate the nations of the Soviet bloc. The Bricker Amendment, which would require domestic legislation before any treaty negotiated by the President could take effect, was the brainstorm of the Republican senator from Ohio. When Bricker's effort failed, a substitute measure having almost the same impact was offered by Democratic Senator Walter George of Georgia. It failed by only a single vote in the Senate.

Late in 1953 Eisenhower became aware of his situation. After less than a year in office he noted that he "had never enjoyed the luxury of being head of a majority party." Although he had earlier excused the intransigence of Republicans in the Congress by noting that they were unfamiliar with the "techniques or the need of cooperating with the Executive," his view had changed radically after only a year's experience. He saw, quite correctly, that the only hope for the future of the Republican party lay in being able "to produce a program that was so dynamic, so forward-looking, and so adapted to the needs of the United States that anyone running as a supporter of the program would have a distinct advantage." Harry S Truman would have agreed. Eisenhower, as a minority party President, had to avoid partisan issues and attitudes.

The election of 1954 ended Republican control of Congress, perhaps permanently. Six years of divided government began with the shift of voters back into Democratic ranks. The electorate, which had trooped happily to the polls to elect Eisenhower, refused to support the heavy campaign he waged for a Republican Congress in 1954. In 1956, while the voters reelected the President by a greater margin than in 1952, they increased the Democratic hold on Congress. The election of 1958 proved to be a landslide for congressional Democrats, and the election of 1960, which saw the Democratic presidential candidate elected by only 118,000 votes, retained heavy Democratic control in both houses of Congress. In only four of the past forty years have Republicans held power in Congress.

CONGRESSIONAL LEADERSHIP OF RAYBURN AND JOHNSON

When the Eighty-fourth Congress convened in 1955, three natives of Texas held the chief positions in the executive and legislative branches. Congressman Sam Rayburn resumed his post as Speaker of the House; and Senator Lyndon B. Johnson became Senate Majority Leader. Of the three native Texans only Eisenhower was philosophically committed to weakening the role of the central government. Neither Rayburn nor Johnson shared the President's fear of federal initiative in solving national problems, nor did they mistrust strong presidential leadership exerted by Democratic Presidents. In 1955, serving with a Republican President, Rayburn and Johnson acted as "congressional" men.

Sam Rayburn was first elected to the United States House of Representatives in 1912, after service as Speaker of the Texas House of Representatives. He moved quietly into the Democratic group of loyalists as a member of the Commerce Committee. He served at all levels of Democratic leadership in the House, and in 1940 he was elected Speaker, a post he held for seventeen years. Throughout these years, Rayburn conducted his "board of education" for newly elected Democrats, telling them that to get along, they would have to go along. Rayburn saw himself not as driver of the House but as its consensual leader, endlessly working to construct a policy around which a Democratic majority could gather. Always intensely partisan, Rayburn had a reputation for complete honesty with supporters and opponents alike, and his personal motivation led him to work for national rather than parochial interests. Enjoying the luxury of a "safe" seat, Rayburn delighted in describing himself as a Democrat "without prefix or suffix."

The Senate Majority Leader, Lyndon B. Johnson, was no less a master of the political process. Elected to the House in 1937, Johnson journeyed immediately to obtain the blessing of Franklin D. Roosevelt, whose yacht was then anchored in Texas waters. From his first days as a member of the House, Johnson was known as a "spokesman for the White House." He was also the student and protégé of Sam Rayburn before moving on to the Senate in 1948. Johnson was elected Senate Minority Leader in 1953 and became Majority Leader when Democrats regained control of Congress. Unlike Rayburn, Johnson was possessed of an endless zeal to lead. From 1955 to 1961, when he took the oath as Vice-President of the United States, Lyndon Johnson was the most powerful man in the Senate. His leadership was based on longer hours of work than any other senator, better information than any other senator, deeper devotion to infinitesimal detail than any other senator, and keener perception of every matter before the Senate than any other senator. Johnson also posssessed an unerring and unforgetting memory for every act of friend or foe in the Senate.

In the Republican Eighty-third Congress Rayburn and Johnson had pursued a policy of cooperation with the President whenever possible. They had never operated as "professional opponents," and in some key votes, as we have noted, they provided the margin for presidential victory. As leaders from 1955 to 1961 Rayburn and Johnson expanded their policy-making role in spite of only nominal majorities in both houses. They exploited the narrowed capacity for policy development which Republican dissent placed on the Republican party and the Republican President. The Democratic leaders conferred frequently with President Eisenhower and proffered support for presidential measures which tended to entrench the social gains of the New Deal and Fair Deal, particularly the extension and broadening of social security legislation. Their objectives were clear: to share as full partners in making national policy; to liberalize administration measures whenever possible; to propose projects which would not draw a presidential veto; and to make a Democratic record capable of enhancing the possibility of electing a Democrat to the presidency.

Rayburn and Johnson were unsuccessful in electing a Democratic President in 1956, as Eisenhower swept to an overwhelming victory over Stevenson. In spite of the Eisenhower sweep, the Democrats increased the strength of their hold on the Senate and maintained themselves in the House. Long before the election of 1956, Eisenhower had begun to concentrate on foreign policy. During his second term he practically abdicated his domestic leadership to Rayburn and Johnson, advocating programs which advanced the "paternalism" he had denounced in 1952 and 1953. His budget for 1958 proposed to spend $72,000,000,000, the largest sum in the nation's peacetime history to that date. Conservatives of both parties engaged in an intensive battle against the President's proposals. Aided by liberal Democrats anxious to embarrass the President, the conservatives forced reductions of over $4,000,000,000 in expenditures. Sharp cuts in spending plus a major downturn in business induced the recession of 1957 and a federal deficit of almost $3,000,-000,000. Fiscal 1959 recorded the largest peacetime deficit ever suffered by the federal government to that date, over $12,400,000,000.

During his second term Eisenhower only occasionally turned his full attention to domestic affairs, seemingly content with the competent leadership of Rayburn and Johnson. The President used his office to protect defense expenditures and foreign aid appropriations, to secure a four-year extension of the reciprocal trade authority, and to reorganize the Defense Department. Rayburn and Johnson, warily guarding against a presidential veto, obtained statehood for both Alaska and Hawaii, retained reduced price supports for staple crops, created the National Aeronautics and Space Agency, and passed a labor union reform act sponsored and managed in the Senate by Senator John F. Kennedy.

Eisenhower's decision to abandon domestic programs for greater attention to foreign policy was not entirely a free choice. The balance of terror with the Soviets remained precarious throughout the Eisenhower years. He also shared his party's desire to "do something" about Asia, particularly following the defeat of the French in Vietnam. Eisenhower also faced the possibility of simultaneous action by the Soviets in Europe and the Chinese or North Koreans in Asia. Knowland might call for war on Red China or Dulles might publish his accounts of "going to the brink," but Eisenhower reserved ultimate foreign policy decisions to himself. Much of his interest in foreign relations was whetted by his inability to move domestically, but most of Eisenhower's concern and activity in foreign affairs was forced by real and proximate threats of war.

EVALUATION OF EISENHOWER'S PRESIDENCY

How shall we assess Dwight David Eisenhower as President of the United States? Eisenhower came to the presidency on an overwhelming vote by his countrymen after a campaign which promised to change the policies of the previous Democratic administrations. It is not surprising that

Eisenhower saw his victory in 1952 as a "mandate for change," an invitation to eradicate the paternalism which he and his fellow campaigners professed to see as a threat to freedom in America. Unable to unify his party in Congress during his first two years in office and faced with growing Democratic domination of the legislative branch, he ultimately helped to consolidate some of the programs he had originally pledged to eliminate. Acquiescing to the legislative leadership of Rayburn and Johnson after 1952, he made sufficient use of his veto power to contain the more liberal tendencies of the Democrats in Congress. He thus allowed only minimal fulfillment of the Truman agenda.

In foreign policy Eisenhower at first appeared bent on changing whatever had been originated by Truman and Acheson. The rhetoric of the Republican campaign of 1952 seems not to have made its impression on Eisenhower until after he had assumed the presidency. Only then did he realize the monstrous nature of the advice he was being given by many of his military and civilian advisers. He tolerated the cries for war against Red China and the recommendations for use of American troops and air power in Vietnam, but he declined to act. In short, he reverted to his education and experience and the latent pacifism common to professional military officers the world over.

During his entire military career Eisenhower offered no challenge to presidential control of the military, and he was content to administer whatever policy he received from Headquarters. His education and experience ill suited him to assume the presidency when he did, because he, in common with his fellow officers, had permitted technology to dull his social sensitivities. In this century, as the result of a revolution in weapons, logistics, and transportation, science has become the tyrant of military combat and professional officers the mere servants of technology. As late as 1952

Eisenhower was a stranger to social concern. He was, as a result, easily attracted to the idle dream of returning to a simpler past.

Eisenhower's strictures on paternalism and his unsophisticated definition of the faults of the New Deal and the Fair Deal must be taken at face value. His denunciation of "politicians" was a carry-over from the lean days of the Army between two wars, when "professionalism" entailed avoidance of interest or participation in any civilian activity. It is no accident that Eisenhower was a member of no political party or organized church until shortly before he became President; his political spectrum was bounded by the Army, and his faith lay in the God so carefully preached by nondenominational Army chaplains. He was a part of the military feudal system between 1915 and 1950 in which every member wore his status on his shoulders and his identity in his regimental insigne. Eisenhower changed little during his presidency.

Eisenhower represented the only political hope of Republicans in 1952, but he had convinced himself that his country needed to be turned away from the "wrong directions" of the New Deal and Fair Deal. He was utterly sincere in his willingness to lead a "crusade" and completely unaware that he was an anachronism in the presidency. Like traditional Presidents before him, he refused to concern himself with policy and contented himself to deal in generalities and platitudes. He saw the presidency as a collection of "power" which he hoped to "return" to the states, not on the basis of rational analysis but as a good idea. He mistook his mandate of 1952 because he was unaware of what the voters wanted. He was neither an intellectual nor a student of civilian politics. From 1953 to 1961 he served as the national "father figure," substituting popular confidence for presidential leadership.

As soldier and President, Eisenhower never failed to respect the status of the presidency, but neither did he demonstrate understanding of the presidential authority. If Roosevelt were a king and Truman an innovator, Eisenhower served best as a regent. After a false start, during which he appeared ready to diminish presidential prerogatives and authority, he defended his office with skill and devotion. He fought the Bricker Amendment, refused to permit congressional probers to subpoena records of the executive branch, and extended presidential immunity to officials and advisers who served him. He declared his right, as commander-in-chief, to dispatch troops in support of his foreign and domestic policy without consent of Congress, and he reorganized executive agencies and departments for efficiency. He resisted all domestic attacks on the presidential institution, and he allowed Rayburn and Johnson to achieve limited social gains. He reacted as well in time of foreign crisis, rejecting out-of-hand outrageous advice, and it was in foreign affairs that he made his best contributions. His experience, his unblemished military record, and his innate caution saved him from military adventures.

Eisenhower was an amiable and popular President, and he retired to Gettysburg, Pennsylvania in 1961 with his reputation largely intact. His balancing influence in a decade marked by shrillness, paranoia, and self-doubt was a priceless contribution. His years as President were blemished, however, by his unwillingness to attack problems which were becoming increasingly more visible. When Eisenhower left the presidency in 1961, a significant part of the American population was living in abject poverty, major cities had reached an advanced state of decay, the national economy was subject to recurring recessions and unemployment, and the military establishment stood incapable of responding to challenges short of nuclear war. Eisenhower also left an unintended legacy to John F. Kennedy—racial problems so long neglected that the slightest spark ignited a major conflagration. Eisenhower failed to employ the presidential authority required to move forward the needed Truman agenda.

NOTES

The Decision to Run: This account of Eisenhower's decision to become a candidate for President is based on the book *Mandate for Change* by Dwight D. Eisenhower (1963). All references to this book made in this chapter are based on the Signet edition (1965), which is available as a paperback.

Political Novice: Eisenhower's claim to be a "political novice" is found on p. 57 of *Mandate for Change*.

Eisenhower in Europe: Eisenhower's account of the defeat of the Axis powers was published in 1948 as *Crusade in Europe*.

Eisenhower vs. New Deal and Fair Deal: Eisenhower's determination to dismantle the work of Roosevelt and Truman is recorded in *Mandate for Change*, pp. 77, 97–98, and especially 152.

Presidential Addresses, 1953: Eisenhower's discussion of his first inaugural address is in *Mandate for Change*, p. 140. For the 1953 State of the Union message, see *Mandate*, pp. 162–165.

The Staff System: Louis W. Koenig, *The Chief Executive* (revised edition, 1968), pp. 167–171, contains an excellent summary of the Eisenhower staff system. Koenig, in his *The Invisible Presidency* (1960), also devotes an entire chapter to charging that Sherman Adams actually ran the presidency. But, given Eisenhower's character, this charge makes little sense.

Vietnam: Eisenhower discusses Vietnam in *Mandate for Change*, pp. 417–429. His assessment of the situation in 1954 is clear evidence of his unwillingness to intervene unless such intervention were decisive. See *Mandate for Change*, pp. 412–413. Eisenhower's high intelligence and ability to reason are attested to in Arthur Krock, *Memoirs: Sixty Years on the Firing Line* (1969), p. 325; Arthur Larson, *Eisenhower* (1968), pp. 168–171; and Emmet J. Hughes, *The Ordeal of Power* (1964). He was never a tool of his advisers, and he made his own decisions, both good and bad.

Eisenhower vs. Congress: Eisenhower's appraisal of his own power to force action by Congress is completely realistic. See *Mandate for Change*, pp. 243–246. The Bricker Amendment controversy is also discussed in *Mandate*, pp. 341–348.

The Republican Congress: For Eisenhower's summary of his accomplishments with the Republican Congress, see *Mandate for Change*, p. 527.

Eisenhower's Political Philosophy: Eisenhower describes his developing political philosophy in *Mandate for Change*, pp. 527–529.

The Housing Proposal: See *Mandate for Change*, p. 360.

China and Korea: Eisenhower evidently believed that his nuclear threat to Red China and North Korea had brought those powers to serious negotiations. Interestingly, he fails to note the death of Stalin as a factor. See *Mandate for Change*, p. 230.

Chiang "Unleashed": Eisenhower used his first State of the Union message to announce the "unleashing" of Chiang. See *Mandate for Change*, p. 164. The "releashing" of Chiang is reported without comment in *Mandate*, p. 564. Chiang agreed with the latter move. Eisenhower explains the new defense policy in detail in *Mandate*, pp. 533–548.

Eisenhower vs. Conservatives: For an account of Eisenhower's difficulties with the conservatives, see Chapter 12 of *Mandate for Change*. Eisenhower's early excuses for the behavior of the Republican conservatives are in *Mandate*, p. 243.

Majority Party Hopes: Eisenhower's diagnosis of what the Republican Party must become if it is to command a majority in Congress is in *Mandate for Change*, pp. 516–517.

Rayburn and Johnson: Eisenhower explains his ability to get along with Rayburn and Johnson in *Mandate for Change*, p. 588.

States' Rights: The sole discussion of states' rights by Eisenhower consists of a four-line paragraph in *Mandate for Change*, p. 256.

American Poverty: Michael Harrington, in *The Other America* (1962), ably describes the advance of poverty in the U.S. during a period which John Kenneth Galbraith described as "The Affluent Society" in 1958.

4. John F. Kennedy: The New Frontier

John Fitzgerald Kennedy, on January 20, 1961, proclaimed to his audience that the "torch has been passed to a new generation of Americans—born in this century, tempered by war, disciplined by a cold and bitter peace, proud of our ancient heritage." He was careful to contrast the optimism of his hopes for the future of the nation with the pessimism of the Eisenhower years by making a direct connection between the youth of the new administration and the objectives of the New Frontier. The inaugural address, employing the language and imagery of American history, was "historic," because he intended it to be so. Kennedy's campaign for the presidency had been based on the theme of getting America moving again toward social and economic growth. The inaugural address, spoken in the rhetoric of stark realism, was nonetheless a demand on the innate idealism of the American people to rededicate the nation to progress.

That Kennedy received the Democratic nomination for the presidency in 1960 is remarkable. He had been projected into national attention by conservatives and southern Democrats during the convention of 1956 as their champion against the liberal Senator Estes Kefauver in the vice-presidential contest. Kennedy was not known as a major liberal leader either in the House or the Senate, although his great popularity in Massachusetts enabled him to defeat Senator Henry Cabot Lodge, Jr., in spite of the Eisenhower sweep of 1952. His liberal credentials suffered further suspicion among those who remembered his father, Joseph P.

Kennedy, as the isolationist ambassador to Britain during Franklin Roosevelt's second term. Service by Robert F. Kennedy as Democratic counsel to the Committee on Government Operations, his apparent cooperation with Senator Joseph R. McCarthy of Wisconsin, and the fact that Ambassador Joseph Kennedy invited McCarthy to the Kennedy home at Hyannisport did nothing to endear John F. Kennedy to liberals of the Democratic party.

In the Senate Kennedy was not fully accepted by the leadership or the senior members. He was too youthful in appearance; he was too independent in his voting; he was too wealthy; he was too well educated; and he was too often absent. Neither was he a "Senate man," in that he ignored the prescribed route of deference and hard work which, combined with seniority, is essential to success in the Senate.

In 1960 the congressional leadership, together with former President Harry S Truman, preferred Stuart Symington or Lyndon Johnson for the presidential nomination. Failing that, they would accept Hubert Humphrey, a "Senate man," although often a combative one. Truly liberal Democrats continued their love affair with the brilliant but quixotic Adlai Stevenson. At the beginning of Kennedy's drive for the nomination, only Governor Abraham A. Ribicoff and National Committeeman John Bailey, both of Connecticut, openly supported the Massachusetts senator.

THE ELECTION OF 1960

Kennedy, however, had certain assets which conditions in 1960 permitted him to use to good advantage. Eisenhower, even if his health had been good and his age were a full decade less, was the first President to be disqualified for renomination by the anti-FDR Twenty-second Amendment to the Constitution. The predictable departure of Eisenhower from the presidency, together with the general Democratic desire to have a crack at Nixon as Eisenhower's putative successor, brought forth a proliferation of candidates. The large number of Democratic contenders in 1960 was to Kennedy's advantage, since none could claim to possess the convention votes necessary for nomination. Success in key primary elections could provide both the essential national exposure and a number of pledged delegate votes for the man who was basically a New England candidate. If Kennedy could demonstrate nationwide appeal to the party membership, he could do much to soften charges that he was too young, too rich, too literate, and too Catholic.

Kennedy made his decision to run for President after the convention of 1956 and proceeded to broaden his political organization for the presidential effort, making contact with young and perceptive politicians throughout the country. His other assets consisted of his own abilities, a brother whose brilliance as a political organizer has seldom been equaled, the considerable family fortune, and the all-consuming desire for public service instilled in him by his parents. Neither John Kennedy nor his campaign manager, Robert F. Kennedy, deluded themselves into thinking that they could win the nomination except on the first ballot. The story of their victory is well known; it is the story of organization, daring, hard work, money, and the personal charm of John F. Kennedy.

The Republican convention of 1960 was well orchestrated to retain what President Eisenhower liked to call "modern Republicanism." Vice-President Nixon, having received the blessing of Eisenhower, made peace with Republican liberals by accepting a platform which went well beyond the Eisenhower practice regarding civil rights and education. Embittered Taftites professed to see a surrender of Republican principles in the platform, and Harold Stassen's reported candidacy offered the necessary comic relief for the convention. Richard M. Nixon's acceptance speech was probably the finest oratorical effort of his entire career. He offered to continue what Eisenhower had been doing so well, but he was manacled by his predecessor's record and unable to promise to do more things or better things or different things. Following Nixon's designation of Henry Cabot Lodge, Jr., to complete the ticket, the Republican candidate became an overwhelming favorite to win the election. Richard M. Nixon, far removed from the day he had answered an advertisement for a candidate to oppose Congressman Jerry Voorhis, had the vital assets of the national administration for his fullest use.

The odds against a Kennedy victory in 1960 were astronomical. Even as the Democrats chose Kennedy on the first ballot and accepted Lyndon B. Johnson for Vice-President; even as Kennedy addressed the delegates, offering to take them forward into the New Frontier; even as they recognized in Kennedy the regal bearing of Roosevelt and the idealism of Truman, many delegates accepted the idea that they had chosen quality over success. Some of the professionals sulked in their tents—Kennedy was too young. Others watched their party nominate a Catholic, a man whom they could not in good conscience support. Some, embittered by the result, talked about the nomination having been bought. In some communities, new political headquarters appeared, emblazoned with the legend "Democrats for Nixon." Throughout the South the Democratic organization fell apart on both the sectional and the religious issues.

Having obtained the nomination, John Kennedy was at once intelligent, dispassionate, detached, and practical. The masterstroke was the choice of Lyndon Johnson as his running mate. Johnson could bring back the professionals; he could influence his congressional colleagues to support the ticket (he was also on the ballot in Texas for reelection to the Senate); and he could campaign in the South. Above all, Lyndon Johnson was loyal; he and Kennedy would fail or triumph together. There was need, respect (never shared by Robert Kennedy), and affection on both sides of the "marriage of convenience" of 1960. Johnson, at Kennedy's request, made an immediate visit to Harry S Truman, who then announced his full support for John F. Kennedy.

Lyndon Johnson always admired a man who understands the political process, a process in which gaining the presidency is the supreme test. Johnson also venerated success, and Kennedy had defeated him in open combat for the nomination. Also, Lyndon Johnson wanted to become President of the United States. But he was fully aware of the anti-Texas sentiment of the Eisenhower years, and he knew that Lyndon Johnson, Texan, stood little chance of success. Only were he to serve eight years with Kennedy in a progressive administration would the Texas disability erode.

The campaign issue, as drawn by Kennedy, was simple: The nation could continue to wallow in mediocrity, failing to live up to its promise, or it could move forward. Americans could follow the true and tested course and accomplish little, or they could risk untried paths and move ahead. The people could be satisfied with minimal progress toward social and political equality, or they could press forward. Kennedy was running against "Eisenhowerism," not against Nixon and most certainly not against Eisenhower. He was calling forth American idealism, the normal American response to challenge, the old faith in the unique morality of this nation, and the vocation of America to lead the world to new heights of peace, justice, and accomplishment.

The long, stabbing finger of John Kennedy moved regularly toward his listeners as he constantly stated his article of faith, "We can do better." In the uphill fight, Lyndon Johnson, at last free of the bonds imposed on him by a conservative constituency, was throwing away his prepared texts and putting on a stem-winding performance of populist oratory unequaled since the 1930s. As they moved across the nation, the old Democracy came alive. Both men were touching the minds, the hearts, and the souls of the voters. Both men believed in the ingrained idealism and progressive thinking of Americans. Neither man had accepted the nomination as an empty gesture; Kennedy and Johnson were determined to win.

Richard Nixon was moving forward in his own way, as his own campaign manager. Inhibited in his campaigning by the Eisenhower record, he resorted to novelties. He promised to visit all fifty states; he made heavy use of newspaper and magazine advertising; and with overconfidence in his skills as a debater, he agreed to meet with Kennedy on nationwide television. He made whistle-stop campaigns through doubtful territories, and he fell victim to bad luck when he injured his knee and had to suspend campaigning temporarily. As Nixon moved across the nation, he pointed out his experience as legislator and executive, and he made full use of his position as Vice-President of the United States.

When the votes were in, Kennedy had won election by a margin of only 118,000 votes over Nixon. Kennedy and Johnson, who had counted on a heavy turnout for victory, polled 8,000,000 votes more than Stevenson had obtained in 1956. The Republican vote for Nixon was down 1,500,000 from the number gained by Eisenhower in that same election. Although Nixon later saw the recession of 1960 as the chief factor in his defeat, he probably lost through his unwillingness to make better use of President Eisenhower. The debates obviously gave Kennedy a national introduction to the voters, and the late appearance of Eisenhower in the Nixon campaign permitted Kennedy to dismiss the intervention as "the rescue squad."

Whether the outcome of the election of 1960 was agreeable or disagreeable, it was a triumph for democracy. More than 69,000,000 Americans voted, dividing their support almost equally between Kennedy and Nixon. Kennedy won the presidency by two tenths of one percent of the votes cast in the closest popular election since 1884. The election of 1960 was a political defeat for Richard Nixon but a tribute to his high personal integrity and a testimony of his faith in the American political system. Under heavy pressure to demand a recount, Nixon congratulated the winner and planned for another day.

KENNEDY'S CABINET
AND WHITE HOUSE STAFF

No hint of a possibly flawed mandate marked the arrival of the New Frontier in Washington, D.C. The New Frontier proclaimed by President Kennedy was reminiscent of the New Deal, as the young leader challenged his followers to "get the nation moving again." Even before election day of 1960 liberal fears of Kennedy's conservative tendencies had withered, and the Kennedy accession brought with it a flood of support. As the legislative proposals of the New Frontier were laid before Congress, it became apparent that Kennedy had reverted to the agenda of the Fair Deal. Due to the President's analytical bent and refusal to engage in fantasy, his proposals were more modest than what Truman had demanded of Congress in 1946 and 1948. But like Truman, Kennedy was willing to make use of presidential authority to intervene in the economy; like Truman he sought the "good life" for every American. Before the last of the ceremonies of inauguration day had ended, many Americans had found a new monarch, and John Kennedy did little to refute their judgment.

Beneath the broad popular approval of the new President, who took obvious pleasure in his role, lay a strong foundation of political realism. Adding emphasis to Kennedy's faith in the United Nations was the choice of Adlai Stevenson as ambassador to lead the United States mission to the United Nations. The cabinet became an amalgam of new and old Democrats and included two Republicans. Appointed as Secretary of State was Dean Rusk of Georgia, an experienced and thoughtful diplomat and scholar. Two cabinet posts went to old-line Democrats: J. Edward Day became Postmaster General, and Luther Hodges was Secretary of Commerce. Day was a longtime Washington, D.C. functionary, while Governor Hodges of North Carolina, not a young man but a liberal Democrat, had campaigned tirelessly in the South. Three "New Frontiersmen" were included: Stewart Udall as Secretary of the Interior, Orville Freeman as Secretary of Agriculture, and Abraham Ribicoff as Secretary of Health, Education, and Welfare.

One of the Republicans, Douglas Dillon, came to the cabinet as a banker liberal enough to understand fiscal and monetary policy but conservative enough to check economic overenthusiasm. That he was acceptable to the financial community and had served Roosevelt, Truman, and Eisenhower enhanced his desirability. Robert McNamara, the other Republican in the cabinet, was widely recognized as a master of the managerial techniques needed to bring the Department of Defense under presidential control.

The nation's leading labor lawyer, Arthur Goldberg, became Secretary of Labor, in recognition of labor's aid in the election and in tribute to Goldberg's outstanding accomplishments as a lawyer and advocate of labor reform. To the important position of Attorney General the President appointed his brother, Robert F. Kennedy. When the President later explained this appointment as an opportunity for a young attorney "to get some experience in government before he goes out to practice law," most Americans applauded this high good humor of John Kennedy. What few appreciated was the formidable competence of the Attorney General and the unbounded confidence which the elder brother placed in his junior. Before the year was out, Americans, particularly those opposed to the administration, began to speak of "the Kennedys."

Unlike the Eisenhower staff, the Kennedy White House had no chief of staff. The President conducted his own staff operations, relying on his brother as a trusted adviser. The Press Secretary, Pierre Salinger, was clearly not a policymaker. Kennedy's senior adviser was Theodore Sorensen, who had long served as Senator Kennedy's administrative assistant. McGeorge Bundy became the White House adviser for national security affairs, because Bundy had recommended himself to Kennedy as a man of brilliance who had served as dean of Harvard College. Arthur Schlesinger, Jr., a bridge to Stevenson liberals as a presidential adviser, was a sometimes student of Latin American affairs but more often an example of the liberal intellect. He had little influence with the President. Kenneth O'Donnell and Lawrence O'Brien, Kennedy's permanent political technicians, soon earned the soubriquet "the Irish Mafia." The worst that may be said of the Kennedy White House staff is that it merely served and failed to innovate; the best is that it served with such intense loyalty and devotion that it became an extension of the Kennedy personality.

RELATIONS WITH CONGRESS

The New Frontier pursued its legislative goals more prudently than did the Fair Deal. Both the President and his congressional liaison leader, Lawrence O'Brien, were aware of the costs of the campaign of 1960. The issue of religion alone had cost twenty-nine liberal Democratic seats in the House. Many Democrats who survived the crushing fight of 1960 returned to office by vastly reduced pluralities. Almost none came to victory because of Kennedy; many were reelected by disassociating themselves from Kennedy's candidacy. The President possessed no political base in the House or Senate other than the loyalty of the leadership and liberals in Congress. The narrowness of support in Congress caused Kennedy to husband his strength for major issues while giving ground on measures patently impossible to pass.

The lack of broad party support for the Democratic President came into full public view within two weeks of the inauguration. Because the House Rules Committee had regularly blocked consideration of liberal measures in the House, Kennedy and Speaker Sam Rayburn determined to add committee members committed to the principle of permitting the House to vote on both liberal and conservative bills. In the sharp fight between the Speaker and Rules Committee Chairman Howard W. Smith, Rayburn was upheld by only five votes. His victory of 217 to 212 was made possible by the support of twenty-two liberal Republicans, while sixty-four Democrats had voted against their Speaker, their President, and their party. Following the Rules Committee fight, it was apparent that the President, even when he made use of full leadership pressure, had no working majority in the House.

Careful management, which employed all the skills of Johnson, Rayburn, O'Brien, and the President, produced paper-thin victories on key measures. The first session of the Eighty-seventh Congress passed the emergency farm bill, the housing bill, urban renewal, aid to depressed areas, and a rise in the hourly minimum wage to $1.25. In 1962, following the death of Rayburn, the conservative coalition successfully turned back major administration measures. The farm bill, federal aid to education, the tax reform bill of 1962, and medical care for the elderly under Social Security fell victim to the obstructionists. Kennedy's only key victory in 1962 was the Trade Expansion Act, which permitted the President to bargain with foreign nations on raising or lowering tariffs.

Unlike Eisenhower, Kennedy refused to abdicate legislative initiative to Congress. He used executive orders to create agencies when Congress was slow to act; he proceeded by executive agreement rather than by treaty; he remained master of his budget by impounding funds he had not requested. Although 1962 demanded much of the President's energy to deal with foreign affairs, he continued to exert every pressure available to him to obtain congressional support. He heaped lavish praise on congressmen who supported him; he used patronage with skill to seek votes for legislation; he appealed to the nation for popular demands on congressmen; but he failed to undo the congressional habits of the previous ten years. Thus, he determined to intervene in the congressional elections of 1962.

His decision was based on several factors, chief of which was his belief that his program was identical with "the national interest." His Democratic majorities in both houses of Congress were "paper majorities," not working majorities. He could not afford the "normal" off-year losses of about forty-six seats in the House and seven in the Senate; rather, he needed to increase his support. He was well aware of the record of presidential failure in the off-year contests, but he could not resist the lure of personal political combat, the surge of the crowds as he appealed to their idealism, and the challenge to succeed where others had failed. After a false start in Harrisburg, Pennsylvania, Kennedy settled into the campaign and traveled 19,000 miles before the Cuban missile crisis foreclosed his effort. House losses were held to four seats, and the Democrats in the Senate actually gained four seats.

The political impact of the Cuban missile crisis cannot be measured accurately in the results of the election. Neither party registered a sweep. Kennedy counted a gain of some ten to a dozen votes in the House in support for his program. Five new Democrats in the Senate—Bayh of Indiana, Nelson of Wisconsin, McGovern of South Dakota, Ribicoff of Connecticut, and Edward Kennedy of Massachusetts—were definite additions to New Frontier strength. Republicans gained four key governorships—New York, Pennsylvania, Ohio, and Michigan—creating four possible opponents for the President in 1964. In California, Governor Edmund Brown handily defeated his opponent, Richard M. Nixon. On balance, the President was pleased.

The Eighty-eighth Congress was more tractable to the presidential lead. For the first time there was noticeable achievement for the New Frontier as President Kennedy offered legislation he had not dared to entrust to the previous Congress. During the spring and summer of 1963, the President signed into law the Mental Health Act, the Higher Education Act, the Maternal and Child Health Act, the Aid to Medical Education Act, the Air Pollution Act, and the law creating the National Cultural Center in Washington, D.C. The last week of September brought approval of the Nuclear Test Ban Treaty in the Senate by a vote of eighty to nineteen, fourteen more votes than the required constitutional majority. But two measures essential to the President's program, the civil rights bill and the tax bill of 1963, remained deeply mired in Congress.

CIVIL RIGHTS

Kennedy's Civil Rights Message to Congress, delivered in February 1963, was typically phrased in terms of both ethical and practical considerations. Discrimination and segregation were wasteful of the talents of people; they divided the nation; and they dishonored our democracy. Worse, he said, such practices were clearly irrational. The President had already used his authority to end discrimination in interstate travel in 1962, and the Attorney General was unceasing in his enforcement of the Civil Rights Acts of 1957 and 1960. President Kennedy had earlier employed executive powers to protect the freedom riders in Alabama, and he had required obedience to federal court orders commanding the University of Mississippi to admit qualified Negro students. The Civil Rights Message demanded equality of rights for all Americans and protection of those rights by workable acts of Congress.

In the spring of 1963 the Southern Christian Leadership Conference, led by Martin Luther King, served a minimal list of demands on the city of Birmingham, Alabama: token employment of Negroes in white businesses, the right for Negroes to eat at lunch counters in stores which did business with Negro customers, and a biracial committee to seek ways to desegregate the school system. Demonstrations were met by savage overreaction from Public Safety Commissioner Eugene Connor. King arrived at Birmingham on Good Friday, April 12, 1963, and was arrested for leading an unauthorized march. Attorney General Robert Kennedy notified city authorities that the national government would tolerate no harm of King in the Birmingham jail, and thousands of additional marchers took up the cause of Negro rights. Network television began extensive coverage of the uncontrolled fury to which demonstrators were subjected, and the nation recoiled in shock and disbelief. The Negro Revolution began at Birmingham in April and spread by May and June to every major city in the nation. It was a revolt of people deprived of their rights in their native land, and in spite of King's avowal of the principle of nonviolence, the revolution was not peaceable in many cities. The summer of 1963 was a time of national crisis.

On June 11, the President determined to act. After a smoldering truce had been arranged at Birmingham, George C. Wallace, Governor of Alabama, notified the White House of his intention to "stand in the doorway" of the University of Alabama to prevent registration by Vivian Malone and James Hood, both Negroes but otherwise qualified. On the morning of June 11, Kennedy issued a proclamation commanding the Governor to comply with the federal court order. The President also called the Thirty-first Infantry Division into federal service, making its troops subject to federal orders. These troops had formally been ordered to Tuscaloosa as members of Alabama's National Guard to prevent the registration of the students. Now, true to their oath, they upheld the orders of the President to tell Governor Wallace to step aside. Within minutes both students were registered.

That evening President Kennedy issued an eloquent appeal to the conscience of the nation. He refused to see civil rights as a sectional, partisan, or legal question, and he insisted, "We are confronted primarily with a moral issue. It is as old as the Scriptures and is as clear as the American Constitution." He called upon Americans to solve the problem, not through legislation alone but "in the homes of every

American." Noting that the time had come for action, Kennedy underscored the need for change which would be "peaceful and constructive for all." New laws were needed at every level to provide "what ought to be possible" for all Americans, regardless of race or color. But he added, "Such is not the case." Should Congress fail to enact legislation, the only remedy open to the Negro lay in the streets. On June 19, 1963, the President sent to Congress a much strengthened civil rights bill. Any political support the President had gathered among southern Democrats for his tax bill now had to be spent, according to his conscience, to warn the nation of the need for protection of civil rights.

ECONOMIC POLICY

Kennedy had inherited a stagnant economy from Eisenhower in 1961, and he used his presidential authority to begin a remedy. He advanced the date of federal payments to various segments of the nation; he called on the Federal Reserve System to reduce interest rates; and he obtained emergency legislation to help farmers weather the recession of 1961. During the Berlin crisis of 1961 he requested an additional $3,400,000,000 for defense spending and successfully resisted demands for a tax increase. The economy refused to respond. Unemployment, which had stood at 6.8 percent of the labor force in 1958, fell to only 5.5 percent when Kennedy took office, but early in 1961 it again rose to 6.7 percent and hovered between 5.5 percent and 5.7 percent through 1962 and into 1963.

Kennedy was no professional economist when he entered the White House. In the Senate he had served on the Labor and Education Committee, which heard testimony from distinguished economists, and he had studied their reports with care. Once elected President, he exercised shrewd judgment in selecting his Council of Economic Advisers. Walter Heller of the University of Minnesota became chairman, aided by James Tobin of Yale and Kermit Gordon of Amherst College. All were interventionists, and all, especially Heller, were practitioners of the post-Keynesian "new economics." They found Kennedy's rational mind keenly receptive to their analytical studies as he sought from them new solutions to the problem of a lagging economy. Kennedy rapidly developed major competence in economics, using his superior intellect to "pick the brains" of his council.

In 1957 the United States had suffered its first large trade deficit, and an average annual deficit of about $4,000,-000,000 in the remaining Eisenhower years was incontrovertible evidence of the deeply troubled state of the national economy. During Eisenhower's second term, Europeans exchanged dollars for some $3,000,000,000 in gold.

By late 1962 the economy was showing signs of turning away from the Eisenhower stagnation. The tax credit for investment in new plants and equipment, which Kennedy had proposed in 1961, became law in 1962. Business taxes fell by $2,500,000,000 in 1963, while annual investment in new plants and equipment passed the $40,000,000,000 level for the first time in American history. But soon it was apparent that the economy was not growing rapidly enough to absorb the inflow of people into the labor market and that training and manpower development programs were useless without jobs for the new or retrained workers. Worse, the inefficiencies and old plants in American industry produced American goods at such high costs that the country was no longer competitive in European markets.

In the 1962 State of the Union address, Kennedy was able to report that the trade deficit had been cut from

$2,000,000,000 in 1960 to one third that amount in 1961. The outflow of gold had been reduced to $500,000,000 in the eleven months before the message. Pressure on the dollar and shrill demands by Europeans that the President devalue the currency continued throughout 1962 and probably helped Kennedy to obtain passage of the Trade Expansion Act of 1962. The act provided unprecedented authority for the President to negotiate tariff reductions of up to 50 percent with foreign trading partners. Each American reduction would be accompanied by a reciprocal cut in foreign tariffs, thus opening markets for American goods. Although the trade deficit was not mastered until 1966, the Trade Expansion Act provided the tool by which success was attained.

Expanded foreign trade alone could not solve the problems of the economy any more than could the business tax credits for new and expanded plants. Stronger intervention was needed, and the President chose the Yale commencement of 1962 to fire his opening gun in the campaign to put an end to the economic illiteracy of Congress and the American people. Accepting an honorary degree with the quip that he now possessed the best of both worlds, "a Harvard education and a Yale degree," the President delivered a lecture denouncing the "labels and clichés" that have hobbled American thinking about economic policy. He denigrated ideological approaches to economics as attitudes by which one could enjoy "the comfort of opinion without the discomfort of thought." In August Kennedy delivered a televised report in which he rejected a temporary tax cut but argued that cutting taxes can be "a sound and effective weapon" under proper circumstances. Through the summer and fall the entire administration hammered home the idea of a tax cut as a stimulant to growth. While opponents hurled charges of "fiscal irresponsibility" (Eisenhower denounced the proposal as "fiscal recklessness") and Chairman Mills demanded tax reform, Kennedy pared domestic civilian spending to the lowest level possible. McNamara was relentless in his search for savings in military procurement.

Many Americans were convinced that the combination of a budget of almost $100,000,000,000, an expected deficit in government receipts, and a tax cut constituted not only economic heresy but financial disaster as well. Few outside the academic community were willing to give serious consideration to the President's proposal. Treasury Secretary Dillon, by stating that a tax cut and deficit spending could stimulate economic growth, lost his credibility with many of his Wall Street colleagues and fellow Republicans. When Walter Heller testified that opposition to the tax cut was founded on the "basic Puritan ethic," countless Americans rushed to the defense of the Puritans. The tax bill passed in the House only through assiduous work by the President, House leadership, and Chairman Mills. In the Senate the bill was deeply mired in economic ignorance. Kennedy was troubled by his inability to get congressional action on the tax bill and the civil rights bill, but he dismissed the doldrum as part of the "flows and ebbs" that constitute life.

THE BAY OF PIGS

Kennedy's inaugural address had touched the heart of the nation, and his popularity immediately rivaled that of Eisenhower. The zest which the new President brought to his task convinced Americans that days of greatness lay ahead. The accession of the young President made such a contrast with the staid, workaday mood of the Eisenhower era that the nation bathed in euphoria and dreams of omnicompetence. But within ninety days of the inaugural, the new hope was blunted by disclosure of the Bay of Pigs incident.

An invasion of Cuba by anti-Castro refugees, approved by the President and financed by the United States, had been an abject failure.

Shortly after the election of 1960, Kennedy had been informed of the invasion plan by Central Intelligence Agency Director Allen Dulles. Dulles and his deputy, Richard Bissell, Jr., gave assurances that the plan had received Eisenhower's approval and that the possibility of failure was well within acceptable limits. The new President approved the plan with two restrictions: it was to employ Cubans only, and United States participation would be limited to plans, equipment, and training. Since Kennedy viewed Castro as the betrayer of the anti-Battista Revolution in Cuba, the order was given to cleanse the invasion forces of all pro-Battista elements. Being wary of the plan, Kennedy had asked for a review of it by the Central Intelligence Agency and the Joint Chiefs of Staff. On receipt of favorable reviews of the military merits of the plan and support for such a stroke from his advisers, Kennedy ordered the invasion to begin.

The operation proved an unmitigated fiasco. The entire attack was botched, and Castro's forces won a crushing victory over the refugees. The origin of the attack in Guatemala, United States support of the effort, and the glaring ineptitude of both plans and execution redounded to the discredit of the United States. Kennedy, in consonance with his view of the President as the officer ultimately responsible to the people, went before a press conference and admitted his error. More than Kennedy's pride had been wagered. He had allowed himself to rely on "experts" whose involvement in the venture had transformed them into salesmen. He had not made the intensive study which would have revealed the insufficiency of every factor in the plan.

Two erroneous assumptions were at the base of the lapse in presidential judgment: Kennedy accepted at face value self-serving refugee testimony that Cuba was ripe for an anti-Castro uprising, and he agreed to a bargain-basement implementation of American foreign policy by foreign nationals. Although a national poll found 83 percent approved of Kennedy's handling of the presidency at the time of the Cuban failure, the President thought otherwise. Never again did he rely on the advice of "experts." Instead, he instituted a study group of his personal advisers to determine means of avoiding future blunders. The military and the Central Intelligence Agency were relegated to roles of collecting information and making studies of military capabilities. The study group, led by Robert Kennedy, became the Executive Committee of the National Security Council, in short form, ExComm. Thus Kennedy replaced the highly structured national security organization created by Dwight Eisenhower. ExComm became the President's advisory group in subsequent crises.

SOVIET RELATIONS AND THE MISSILE CRISIS

The Bay of Pigs also played a role in the later and more dangerous confrontation of the United States and the Soviet Union in 1962. Kennedy's inauguration had brought Soviet initiatives for a meeting between Kennedy and Chairman Nikita Khrushchev. Since the President wanted to assess Khrushchev, he agreed to a meeting at Vienna in early June 1961. The conference took place less than two months after the Bay of Pigs, and the Cuban failure was an obvious factor in Khrushchev's reported estimation of the President as a bright, inexperienced, and possibly irresolute leader of the free world. At Vienna the Soviet Chairman agreed that Laos was not worth a Soviet-American war, refused to agree to a ban on atmospheric testing of nuclear warheads, and reiterated his determination to impose a Soviet solution on all of Berlin.

After the conference ended, the Chairman met with his allies in East Germany and assured them of his continued support. Evidence of the Khrushchev assessment of Kennedy was not slow to come. In spite of the President's nationally televised speech on July 25, declaring America's resolution to defend West Berlin, the East German government chose, on August 13, to build a wall dividing East and West Berlin. The wall was, in reality, a confession of East Germany's inability to retain her more productive citizens, but it is doubtful that Moscow saw it that way. Kennedy determined on a show of force at Berlin and requested Vice-President Johnson to fly there. A regimental combat team of the Eighth Infantry Division, some 1,500 troops, crossed East Germany in convoy and arrived in the beleaguered city to be greeted and reviewed by the Vice-President. Thus, in the crisis summer of 1961, the United States reasserted its right to both presence in and access to Berlin, a right gained from the defeat of Nazi Germany.

There is no way to plumb Khrushchev's thinking, but the Bay of Pigs fiasco, the Vienna conference, and the Berlin wall seem all of a piece. If so, they were basic to the miscalculation made by the Soviet Chairman in 1962. Late in August 1962, when the President was heavily engaged in the election of 1962, overflights of Cuba by reconnaissance aircraft provided evidence of major Soviet activity to install missiles, build secure warhead storage points, and erect electronic control facilities for the missiles. Soviet activities in transporting missiles, training personnel, and installing antiaircraft batteries had been monitored throughout the late spring and early summer, but the Soviet ambassador denied that any offensive capability was being supplied to Castro. By early October it was apparent that Cuba was the site of a major installation of Soviet missiles capable of striking the United States a fatal blow. On October 14, clear photographs of the missile sites confirmed that installation of the missiles and their equipment was rapidly taking place, even before an adequate system of antiaircraft protection had been deployed.

Various theories have been advanced in an attempt to account for the Soviet decision to emplace the missiles in Cuba. In essence, whatever the rationale of the Kremlin or the Soviet General Staff, the move was founded in miscalculation. They failed to measure properly the reaction of the President and the American people to their thrust. Put simply, Khrushchev was aware that the Cuban installations were well within the defense perimeters of the United States and presented an intolerable threat. The decision to emplace the missiles was either audacious or stupid, depending on Soviet projections of American reaction. Khrushchev had not survived the vicissitudes of Communist party politics nor become chairman of the Council of Ministers of the Soviet Union on the basis of stupidity.

Khrushchev had miscalculated. It was Khrushchev who recoiled from nuclear confrontation offered by Kennedy. It was Kennedy who bested Khrushchev in the test of strength; and it was Kennedy's perceptive use of military power which bent Khrushchev to the American President's will. The thirteen days of nuclear crisis found America's North Atlantic Treaty Organization allies and the Organization of American States, less Cuba, standing solidly with American policy. More important was the unity of American men, women, and children when the President informed them that they faced nuclear holocaust. What role Khrushchev's Cuban failure played in his downfall is not certain, but Soviet respect for Kennedy had grown immeasurably by June 1963, when the President stood before the Berlin city hall and taunted the

Communist claim to be the wave of the future with his invitation, "Lasst sie nach Berlin kommen."

KENNEDY'S ASSASSINATION

No mortal knew in 1963 that the President's days were numbered, that by an irony of fate his rational leadership would be destroyed by an irrational act. In the fall of 1963 it became increasingly probable that Kennedy's Republican opponent in the next presidential election would be Senator Barry Goldwater of Arizona, an attractive and honest man, whose attitudes toward the nation made a perfect contrast to Kennedy's political views. The Nuclear Test Ban Treaty had gained overwhelming approval in the Senate, and the only real cloud on the horizon came on November 1, when President Ngo Dinh Diem of South Vietnam was overthrown and murdered. Kennedy was saddened by his own tacit role in failing to prevent the coup, and he was shocked by the senseless butchery of Diem and his brother, Ngo Dinh Nhu. Within the week Kennedy recognized, however unhappily, the new dictatorship by the generals at Saigon.

On November 13, the President held a meeting of his political advisers at the White House to phrase the call for the Democratic National Convention of 1964 and to devise some means of making the proceedings interesting. Kennedy told the advisers that he planned to campaign in Florida and Texas, test his prospects in the South, and meet with them again in two to three weeks. On November 22, in the midst of a huge turnout at Dallas, President Kennedy was shot in the head and died almost instantly. For a few moments the nation resisted the news and then plunged into mourning, remorse, and self-pity. As knowledge of Kennedy's death spread through the world, life was suspended for Americans, and the nation temporarily stopped functioning.

EVALUATION OF
KENNEDY'S PRESIDENCY

How shall we assess John Fitzgerald Kennedy as President of the United States? He was handsome, urbane, witty, well-spoken, and attractive. For most Americans his regal bearing, his dignified assumption of the presidential authority, his obvious pleasure in taking up the leadership of the nation, and his ability to create an instant mood of national optimism marked him as the new monarch. Foreigners saw in Kennedy the best that America had to offer, an idealized version of the legendary American living in the land of opportunity. The President's enemies insisted that his charisma was merely a facade behind which lurked a stark lust for power, power ruthlessly gained through lavish use of money.

President Kennedy was much more than his image. He had sought power because he understood its uses; he intended to benefit his country. His mind was that of a disciplined planner who permits himself few impulsive decisions. He was Aristotelian in his pursuit of excellence, and he attempted to blend moderation with progress toward achievable goals. Although Kennedy has been described variously as a pragmatist and an idealist, he was neither. He saw himself and his nation in terms of unblinking realism, and he subjected every problem or project to rational analysis. Accordingly, he tended to tailor his goals not in terms of what was attainable but in the light of what was both valuable and attainable. His demands on Congress were often less striking than those of the Fair Deal, causing some liberals to question the nature of the New Frontier.

Kennedy chose his objectives largely on the strength of his personal convictions. His speeches and messages abounded with ethical terms regarding what ought and ought not to be. The President was the captive of no ideology except the recognition of reason tempered by realism. War, poverty, an underproductive economy, racial discrimination, waste or dishonesty in government or industry—all were irrational and ethically unacceptable to the President. He was detached, analytical in nature, and sometimes cold in his approach to problems. He was no radical. His concern for the poor, the unemployed, and the minorities sprang from compassion, pity, and dismay that such irrationalities continued to exist. But because he sought mastery of his situation, he refused to base his decisions on emotion.

Kennedy achieved full identity as a liberal only after he had become President. He grew rapidly in office, and by the time of his meeting with Khrushchev at Vienna he had developed a completely controlled intellect capable of dissecting policy questions with unusual rigor. With his intellectual ability he combined a warm and engaging personality. He could laugh at himself, make light of personal and political attacks on himself and his family, and deliver speeches which blended a rapier wit with serious discussion. In his press conferences he dominated the stage by his depth of information, readiness to answer questions, and extemporaneous humor.

Kennedy sought no millennium. Rather, he wanted to change the circumstances of American life on a sensible basis. He worked for international cooperation among nations as a substitute for war, and his thrust for détente with the Soviets foresaw an end to the wasteful expenditure of resources by both sides for heavy armaments. The President wanted to eliminate the inefficiencies of the national economy, because he viewed the recurrent cycle of prosperity and recession as a block to the better life for all Americans. His overriding social objective envisioned a social system which offered respect for the individual citizen as well as equality of opportunity for each person to develop his own talents. In sum, President Kennedy labored to eradicate irrational barriers which prevented both individual and national growth.

Kennedy's effectiveness as President is often confused by his great popularity. In preparing to assume presidential authority, he measured his congressional support and concluded that his original objectives must be more circumscribed than those of Truman. As a realist and student of political possibilities he knew his limitations and the need to husband his legislative strength. He plunged into the elections of 1962 in quest of the working majority in Congress denied him in 1960, the majority essential to passage of his program. He fully expected to sweep the election of 1964, exchange his popularity for the coin of political success, and carry with him a Congress ready to support the New Frontier. What the New Frontier was on the verge of being in 1963 we shall now never know.

John F. Kennedy assumed presidential authority with both confidence and relish. He made full use of his authority in the absence of strong congressional support for his programs. He created the Peace Corps by executive order; he used a presidential proclamation to order Governor Wallace to cease his resistance to the federal courts; he employed a blockade of Cuba in 1962 without seeking congressional consent; and he dispatched American troops to Thailand on his own decision. He offered the prestige of his office in the steelworkers' wage settlement of 1962 and mobilized popular support to force a rollback of unwarranted steel price increases. He entered into the Geneva Accord on Laos by executive agreement, and he was unceasing in his use of the Justice Department to enforce the civil rights laws of 1957 and 1960 in spite of congressional hostility. As an activist, President Kennedy proposed and defended the unorthodox tax bill of 1963 in defiance of popular as well as congressional economic ignorance.

Kennedy was constantly on the search for information. He sought advice but made his own decisions in both domestic and foreign policy. He was master in the White House, and he accepted the responsibility for failure with almost as much grace as he showed in receiving the praises of success. His policies were primarily the product of his own conscience, as he sought to establish the primacy of domestic affairs over foreign concerns. He read constantly to inform himself, and he was completely intolerant of imprecise thinking or overblown hopes for success. He gained the ultimate accolade as President when he became the target of hate books published by reactionary authors, a certain sign that he was making his mark on American history by improving the quality of American life.

John Fitzgerald Kennedy does not rank among the great Presidents of the United States. His potential was forestalled by events and circumstances. His support in Congress never equaled that accorded him by the public. (Shortly after the Bay of Pigs, fully 83 percent of Americans approved Kennedy's conduct of his office, while his popularity reached a low of 61 percent approval during the 1963 fight over civil rights and the tax cut.) President Kennedy was also kept from the ranks of the great by the time and energy demanded of him by foreign affairs. Each international flash point seemed to intensify for Kennedy. Cuba, Laos, Berlin, and Vietnam —all came to full blaze and required solutions. To Kennedy's chagrin, foreign problems drained away much of the domestic attention vital to success for the domestic programs of the New Frontier. Congressmen could valiantly vote billions for defense but not one cent for progress.

Kennedy's potential for greatness was finally smashed at Dallas. His time had been too short. Had he served two terms, his capacity for rational decision and the unblushing love of the American people for John F. Kennedy might have provided the opportunity for him to achieve greatness. Events at Dallas robbed Kennedy of his chance to achieve his goals in public service. That a madman had killed the President was no comfort. The stabbing finger, the full smile, the ebullient confidence openly stated, the eloquent speeches endlessly quoted, the elegance of manner, the keenness of wit, the dignity in time of success or failure, and the sense of American primacy which Kennedy personified at home and abroad —all were blasted away at Dallas. The deed was not murder; it was regicide.

What Kennedy sought to achieve as President of the United States is best summarized in his inaugural address, in which he called on his countrymen to join in a struggle against "the common enemies of man: tyranny, poverty, disease, and war itself." Before journeying to Washington, D.C. to assume the presidency, Kennedy had also addressed the legislature of Massachusetts. After praising the Bay Colony and the Commonwealth of Massachusetts as the source of his heritage, Kennedy proposed four tests by which history might judge public men: Were we truly men of courage? Were we truly men of judgment? Were we truly men of integrity? Were we truly men of dedication? John F. Kennedy measured up to his standards even if he did not achieve his goals.

The final sentence of the address with which he assumed the presidency provides a fitting epitaph:

> *With a good conscience our only sure reward, with history the final judge of our deeds, let us go forth to serve the land we love, asking His blessings and His help, but knowing that here on earth God's work must truly be our own.*

NOTES

JFK Biographies: The Kennedy literature is already voluminous, ranging from trivia to serious analysis. The best studies now available are Theodore C. Sorensen, *Kennedy* (1965); Arthur M. Schlesinger, Jr., *A Thousand Days* (1965); and Hugh Sidey, *JFK* (1964). These three constitute the factual basis of this chapter.

Campaign and 1960 Election: The standard reference for the campaign and election of 1960 is Theodore H. White, *The Making of the President, 1960* (1961). For the use of primaries as a tool to force party regulars to support Kennedy's "outside" candidacy, see p. 166.

White House Staff: On the problems of forming the cabinet and staff, see *A Thousand Days*, pp. 127–155. An excellent study of the Kennedy staff is in Patrick Anderson, *The President's Men* (1969), Chapter 5.

Rules Committee Conflict: Nelson H. Polsby, ed., in *Congressional Behavior* (1971), pp. 216–221, gives an excellent short study of the Rules Committee fight of 1961. Tom Wicker, *JFK and LBJ* (1968), concludes that the President won the fight and lost the Congress, but it is difficult to see how Kennedy could have lost what he never had, i.e., the support of Congress.

1962 Elections: *JFK,* pp. 354–364, is an excellent short account of Kennedy's intervention in the elections of 1962.

Civil Rights: Kennedy's general interest in equal rights for all Americans was quickened during the inaugural parade of 1961, when he noted the lily-white Corps of Cadets of the United States Coast Guard Academy and determined to change the situation. Within six months the Academy had its first Negro cadet. He completed his education at the Academy, was commissioned in the regular establishment, and is still on active duty. Sorensen, in *Kennedy,* pp. 473–506, details the civil rights actions of Kennedy. See also *JFK,* pp. 399–402.

JFK and Economics: For Kennedy's economic views, see *Kennedy,* pp. 393–469. *A Thousand Days,* pp. 644–656, provides a short summary of the development of Kennedy's economic policies. *JFK,* Chapter 27, describes Kennedy's mastery of the "new economics." Eisenhower's comment on Kennedy's policy is in *Kennedy,* p. 431; and Heller's "basic Puritan ethic" is in *A Thousand Days,* p. 1,004.

Bay of Pigs: Sidey, *JFK,* pp. 12–13, fixes the date of Kennedy's first knowledge of the Bay of Pigs plan as November 18, 1960. Kennedy's subsequent decision to avoid "experts" and rely on personal advisers is in *A Thousand Days,* p. 296. The President eventually extended this attitude toward the entire bureaucracy; see Louis W. Koenig, *The Chief Executive* (revised edition, 1968), p. 159. Sidey, *JFK,* p. 156, notes Kennedy's popularity at the time of the Bay of Pigs at 83 percent public approval and Kennedy's reply, "My God. It's as bad as Eisenhower."

Cuban Missile Crisis: The best study of the Cuban missile crisis is Robert Kennedy's *Thirteen Days* (1968), particularly in its account of decisions made and the reasons for them. Sorensen, *Kennedy,* pp. 704–709, reports the unity of the American people and the support of NATO and OAS. The most perceptive study of the decisions of Kennedy and Khrushchev is Graham T. Allison, *Essence of Decision* (1971).

Reelection Hopes: Sidey, *JFK,* pp. 419–423, reports Kennedy's last political meeting and the optimism which accompanied it.

JFK—Pragmatist or Idealist? Schlesinger, *A Thousand Days,* pp. 104–113, writes of Kennedy's intellect and describes the President as a pragmatist. This view does not accord with Kennedy's blending of reason with personal convictions of honor and decency. For example, the idea of landing an American on the moon "before this decade is out" was part of a Kennedy Special Message to Congress on May 25, 1961, aimed at rebuilding American technological primacy at the same time the nation undertook important humanitarian research in space.

Presidential Popularity: Kennedy's popularity, measured by any poll, was outstanding. In the summer of 1963, some 59 percent of a sample of voters said they had voted for him in 1960, and after the assassination, 65 percent reported they had supported him in 1960. See P. B. Sheatsley and J. J. Feldman, "The Assassination of President Kennedy: A Preliminary Report on Public Reaction and Behavior,"

Public Opinion Quarterly (Summer 1964). In 1960, Kennedy actually polled 49.5 percent of all votes cast.

Presidential Grace: In his personal life and in his "nonpublic" hours as President, Kennedy reacted as any normal man to failure or personal attacks, often in colorful and highly developed vocabulary. His only public lapse came in the confrontation with Roger Blough, when he remarked, "My father always told me they were sons of bitches." Sidey, *JFK*, p. 294n, reports Kennedy's press conference rejoinder that his father had "on other occasions not [been] wholly wrong."

Reactionary Retaliation: Two hate books are representative of the type: Frank Kluckhohn, *America: Listen!* (1962, 1963); and John A. Stormer, *None Dare Call It Treason* (1964), which became a Goldwater campaign weapon in 1964. At prices of 95¢ for the Kluckhohn book and 75¢ for Stormer's effort, neither was a bargain.

5. Lyndon B. Johnson: The Great Society

The Constitution of the United States permits no inter-regnum or period when the nation is without a President. Following the death of President Kennedy, Lyndon Johnson spoke by telephone with Attorney General Robert Kennedy in Washington, D.C. and decided to take the presidential oath of office before leaving Dallas to return to the capital. So unforeseen were the events at Dallas that the form of the oath had to be located, dictated over the phone, and copied on board Air Force One at Love Field. Judge Sarah T. Hughes of the federal court was located, and she administered the oath. President Johnson gruffly ordered the plane to take off for Washington, D.C.

Confusion regarding the oath of office was part of the shock felt that day in Washington, D.C., Dallas, and every city and town in America. Everywhere there was sorrow, bitterness, horror, and confusion. Each American sought his own understanding of the regicide. Some saw the killing as a Communist plot, carefully orchestrated by Moscow in retaliation for Khrushchev's humiliation in the Cuban missile crisis. Early reports even had it that men of the Right in Dallas, a hotbed of cannibalistic reactionary movements, had planned the murder. (Only a few weeks earlier, United Nations Ambassador Adlai Stevenson had been struck by a picketer's sign at a Dallas meeting to celebrate United Nations Day. In 1960 Lyndon Johnson and Mrs. Johnson arrived in Dallas after a friendly campaign rally in Arlington, Texas, only to be spat upon and threatened by an ugly crowd.) The nation's armed forces were placed on the alert, rumors spread nationwide, and erroneous news reports were common.

When the presidential plane arrived in Washington, D.C., the body of John Kennedy was taken to Naval Medical School at Bethesda, Maryland, where a rigorous autopsy was performed. Mrs. Kennedy and Robert Kennedy rode with the dead President to Bethesda, while Mrs. Johnson accompanied her husband to the White House. The new President went to his vice-presidential office in the Executive Office Building, where he worked until nine that evening. Johnson had learned of Kennedy's death when Kenneth O'Donnell notified him at Parkland Hospital, but the reality of the transfer of power came only when the walking courier, carrying the "football," entered Johnson's room at the hospital. The football, far less dignified than an orb and scepter, is a plain briefcase which symbolizes presidential authority. The case, always in the direct presence of the President when he travels away from Washington, D.C., contains the codes needed to initiate a nuclear strike or to order various levels of military activity. Such is the ironic symbol of leadership in a nation whose self-imposed task is to lead the world in the ways of peace.

Between Friday noon and the following Monday the nation underwent four days of searing agony: the murder of a Dallas policeman, the arrest of Kennedy's assailant, the slaying of the assassin by the owner of a sleazy Dallas nightclub just as President Kennedy's body was being transferred to the rotunda of the Capitol, the endless lines of Americans weeping openly and unashamed, the tight security of the funeral procession, the dignity of the President's widow, the ancient rites performed by the cardinal, the riderless charger, and the solemn interment at Arlington National Cemetery. Not playing a leading role but demonstrating to the world the continuity of the presidential office was the new President of the United States, Lyndon B. Johnson.

Thirty days of official mourning were proclaimed, but there was little need for the action. Churches of every faith and denomination were filled; businesses simply closed; most athletic events were canceled; radio and television broadcast no commercials; cities and highways were almost deserted. The people mourned, at home or in church, and every American understood that he had been cheated of part of his heritage. Like other Americans, Lyndon Johnson felt a sharp sense of personal loss, deepened by his warm friendship for the widow and her children and by the fact that the murder had occurred in Texas. Unlike his fellow citizens, Johnson had to conduct the affairs of government during this period of national sorrow.

No royal cortege in history counted such heartfelt homage as that given to John F. Kennedy by foreign leaders and their people. Emperors, kings, dictators, diplomats, democrats, fascists, communists, warriors, men of peace—all came to pay tribute to the young monarch cut down in his prime, his work unfinished. Being men of affairs, they also came to meet and assess the successor even as they mourned Kennedy's death. They found a man in deep sorrow, polite, obviously in charge, but reticent. He had lost his leader and a friend for whom he held great respect and affection. Worse, he had succeeded to the office as the direct result of a monstrous deed, and he was not prepared for such an eventuality. He did what he could. He asked the Kennedy cabinet and staff to stay on with him, and he conducted essential business which could not be put off. He waited a decent interval to permit the Kennedy family to vacate the White House.

What Johnson could not do was postpone his assumption of the presidential authority and leave the nation leaderless. On November 27, President Johnson addressed a joint session of Congress. His message, short, emotional, and pointed, was carried throughout the nation by radio and television. Lyndon Johnson, he told the Congress, had acceded to the presidency when the man who had been elected had not lived to achieve his policies and programs. Determined to capitalize on popular support of the Kennedy programs and to use the regicide as a goad to Congress, Johnson called on his former colleagues to give President Kennedy his due— pass his program and get the country moving again. Misunderstanding found no place in Johnson's address; he wanted action, and he proposed to get it. All of the old skills and knowledge which had made Lyndon Johnson one of the great leaders of the Senate were brought to bear in the drive to enact Kennedy's program "as a living memorial" to the dead President: "Today, in this moment of new resolve, I would say to all my fellow Americans—let us continue."

JOHNSON'S CONGRESSIONAL CAREER

As President of the United States, Lyndon Johnson achieved what he had never known before, complete political security. As a Texas politician Johnson had been torn by two conflicting forces: his basic political urge toward populism and his realistic need to obtain the support of the great corporate and financial interests in Texas. Texas, with its separate constituencies of conflicting desires and needs and its huge distances to be covered in campaigning; the decreasing power of agriculture after World War II; and Johnson's personal inclinations required him to walk a political tightrope. The tale of Johnson's success in Texas politics is more the story of a survivor than that of a master politician sweeping to victory. At times he took the liberal course, but for the most part he played the conservative role. Johnson refused to become part of the conservative coalition in the Senate, but he looked upon laws providing tax benefits to oil and gas producers as holy writ.

Permanent political power in Texas was denied to Lyndon Johnson, because the conservatives knew he was not one of them. Unlike Shivers, Daniel, Connally, and later Marvin Watson, Johnson was unwilling to accept the nineteenth-century economic philosophy openly espoused by Texas conservatives. Until 1960 there were few admitted Republicans in Texas, and the Democratic party served as a political "Mother Hubbard," covering everything. Johnson's record of cooperation with the new money in Texas was checkered. He voted for the Taft-Hartley Act, and he helped to override Truman's veto, but he also supported increases in the minimum wage law. He was unsparing in his efforts to protect the oil and gas depletion allowances, but in 1959 he blocked confirmation of Lewis Strauss, a vocal and arrogant conservative, to be Secretary of Commerce. Worse, he prevented Senate passage of the blatantly antilabor Landrum-Griffin bill and substituted for it the labor reform bill managed in the Senate by John F. Kennedy.

Much of the masterful "wheeling and dealing" style of Johnson's leadership of the Senate was an attempt to add security to his shaky Texas base. If the conservatives failed to trust Johnson, his endless maneuvering and coalition-building made Texas liberals wary of him. Johnson's Tenth Congressional District, which he represented from 1937 to 1948, was basically liberal. It contained Austin and the University of Texas, the large Mexican-American city of San Antonio, and the hill country west of Austin where populism still had its greatest strength in Texas. Johnson, never really poor but born into a family of dirt farmers and populist politicians, learned the doctrines of frontier radicalism at his father's knee. In the House, Johnson could represent his district, vote his convictions, and remain a loyal follower of Sam Rayburn and the New Deal.

In 1941 Lyndon Johnson offered his candidacy for the Senate in an announcement made from the steps of the White House. In spite of political support from Rayburn and Roosevelt and Johnson's complete devotion to the New Deal, he was defeated by 1,311 votes. The liberal principles so thoroughly accepted in the Tenth Congressional District had far less appeal statewide. The new money in Texas, derived from oil and gas production, was fast replacing agriculture in importance and demanding political power. In 1944 the new conservatives attempted to defeat Speaker Sam Rayburn and posed such a threat to him that he remained in his district to campaign rather than join the national effort for Roosevelt. By 1948 Johnson had made his peace with the conservatives but won election to the Senate by only eighty-seven of over 900,000 votes cast. When the narrow victory was challenged, the entire Truman administration successfully entered the fight to seat Lyndon Johnson. Although Johnson had carefully disassociated himself from Truman during the campaign, the President was unwilling to tolerate Johnson's Dixiecrat opponent.

Johnson, as Minority Leader of the Senate, was elected to his second term in 1954 as defender of the Democratic party. Senator Joseph R. McCarthy had coined a slogan to describe the Roosevelt-Truman years—"twenty years of treason"—and other Republicans had foolishly taken up the cry. Johnson came forth as the champion of his party, campaigned nationally but seldom in Texas, and won handily. His conservative opponent, wealthy but eccentric, was overwhelmed. In mid 1956 Johnson cooperated with Speaker Rayburn and other Texas liberals to prevent a repeat of the presidential campaign of 1952, when most of the Democratic organization had campaigned for Eisenhower. Having defeated Governor Shivers and the conservatives, Johnson then refused to force out the Shivers-appointed members of the Democratic Executive Committee. While liberals fumed, Johnson declared himself the favorite-son presidential candidate of Texas.

Rayburn would have no part of Johnson's semiserious quest for the presidential nomination. Not only was the Speaker the elected chairman of the convention of 1956, but he was also convinced that Adlai Stevenson already had the nomination locked up. Stevenson did win the nomination without real opposition and then surprised the delegates by throwing open the choice of a vice-presidential nominee. Johnson nursed some hope of gaining selection himself, but he was committed to Hubert Humphrey as second choice. To Johnson's chagrin he learned that the Texas delegation supported the candidate of the conservative South, Senator John F. Kennedy. Johnson moved quickly as leader of his delegation to cast fifty-six votes for "the fighting sailor who wears the scars of battle."

Lyndon Johnson, in 1960, wanted to be named the candidate of the Democratic convention for President of the United States. In this Rayburn backed him, not only due to the Speaker's unconcealed hatred of Richard M. Nixon, but because Rayburn was honestly afraid that a Catholic nominee would guarantee Democratic defeat. Johnson sought the nomination from his only secure power base, the United States Senate. He refused to enter the primaries or make speeches, pledging his devotion to the Senate. He failed to announce his candidacy for the nomination until July 5, apparently believing that his power over the Senate could give him control of the convention. Earlier, Rayburn and Johnson had hoped that Kennedy and Humphrey would destroy each other as candidates, but Humphrey had failed to survive. At the Democratic convention of 1960 the "stop Kennedy" movement of Johnson and the other candidates also failed. Kennedy achieved nomination on the first ballot. If Johnson were ever to gain the presidency, he would need a national constituency, not the shaky and formless vendetta which passes for Democratic politics in Texas. Thus Johnson accepted the vice-presidential nomination and provided the key to a Kennedy-Johnson victory.

PRESIDENTIAL RELATIONS WITH CONGRESS

As he had indicated in his first speech to Congress, President Johnson wanted continuity of the Kennedy policies, and he rejected congressional resistance to Kennedy. Johnson's experience with Congress had left him little respect for either House or Senate. He professed his great love for his "former colleagues," and he spoke often of Congress as "my home," but he drove the Congress without mercy or restraint. Once again, as in his days as Majority Leader, Lyndon Johnson knew where the bodies were buried and where the lines of real power lay. He knew also the uses to which the almost mystical popularity of the dead President might be put, were someone bold enough to employ it. To all this Johnson added the presidential authority which was now his. More important for the nation, Lyndon Johnson was at last free from the restraints which Texas had imposed on him throughout his career, free to follow his own political convictions.

In his dealings with the Eighty-eighth Congress, President Johnson played a shifting role. Whenever the occasion offered opportunity to render public praise of members of Congress, Johnson was in the forefront, leading the applause.

The doors of the White House were open to congressmen and senators, and many Americans saw Lyndon Johnson as the perfect partner for a productive legislature. Beyond the public's view, however, the President intervened in congressional affairs to an extent unprecedented in this century. The civil rights bill, the tax bill, the poverty bill, and the upwardly adjusted foreign aid bill—all became law after passage by both houses and signature by the President. Johnson worked the Congress without pause, demanding that all appropriations measures be enacted by December and that the sale of American wheat to the Soviet Union be approved. When Kennedy had made this proposal in October, the conservative coalition prepared to block the supposed "aid to Communists" by forbidding the Export-Import Bank to make available the necessary foreign exchange. Using all his skills, the new President held the weary Congress in session and ordered an unprecedented Christmas Eve vote on the foreign aid bill, which contained no restriction on the sale of wheat to the Soviets. Marking the end of the official period of mourning for President Kennedy, Johnson held a party at the White House for more than 200 congressmen. Less than one day later the President had his way; the bill was passed.

Even as Johnson was obtaining passage of the Kennedy program, he was acting to contain his opponents. As we have seen, the coalition of Republicans and southern Democrats opposed almost every liberal project of Roosevelt, Truman, Eisenhower, and Kennedy. In most cases the key to the conservative opposition was fear of rising federal expenditures. Johnson was not, himself, immune to fears of profligate spending, but he brought to the White House a view of the central government as the sole impartial tool capable of working justice for every citizen. If funds were to be available to do the government's work, strict economy was a necessity, and Johnson began work immediately to cut the budget tentatively approved by Kennedy. Neither was Johnson immediately enthusiastic about the tax bill of 1964 because of its unorthodox economic doctrine. After hours of conferring with Dillon, Heller, and Budget Director Gordon, Johnson agreed to support the tax bill and to combine with it a promise to cut spending by $1,500,000,000. When the conferences ended, Johnson concluded that Heller and Dillon had educated him in the "new economics" while he had educated them in politics.

LYNDON JOHNSON AND POPULISM

Johnson's political convictions included not only respect for a dollar but a refinement of the frontier radicalism of the populist era. The frontier radical honestly believes that he is no radical at all but the true heir to traditional American values. He places great faith in equality of opportunity for all Americans and the enduring worth of work. He stands foursquare on Jefferson's words in the Declaration of Independence, "All men are created equal." The frontier radical believes in prosperity for all Americans through the proper distribution of the riches of the nation. The frontier radical analysis, not easily refuted by historical references, is that monopoly, economic and political combinations, unfair advantage gained by some Americans, or simple injustice prevents prosperity for all.

Earlier populists held the same views of American life, but the narrowness of their views and the intensity of their battles against enemies such as railroads and banks prevented them from making a wholly rational argument for their stand. The populism of the late nineteenth century was based in emotion and deeply held beliefs and fell victim, in many cases, to blatant racism. The populists could, accordingly, be dismissed as eccentrics, zealots, and anti-intellectuals. Modern populists, though clinging to the radical analysis of the economic system, have thrown off both the racism and anti-intellectualism which doomed their predecessors. Huey P. Long, Harry S Truman, and Lyndon B. Johnson form the vanguard of modern populism. Their youthful experience came in an era of business domination of government in a land of arrangements, monopolies, combinations, and injustices hallowed by tradition into law.

Huey Long led a battle to liberate the people and the resources of Louisiana from an incredible web of monopoly and theft, only to lose his reputation and life to his heavy-handed political operations. Long, never a racist, further smeared his excellent achievements for Louisiana by his political flirtations with two clergymen, Father Charles E. Coughlin and Gerald L. K. Smith. Coughlin, an anti-Semite, and Smith, a Negro-hater, eventually developed a naïve brand of American fascism. Truman, originally elected a county administrator, translated his modern populist principles into the Fair Deal and created the contemporary presidency as a necessary administrative tool. Johnson, so long held in thralldom by the new money in Texas, used the presidential authority to advance his populist goals.

Modern populists seldom admit to being populists, probably because of the racism and anti-intellectual qualities of the early populists. In general the modern frontier radicals refer to themselves as liberals, although they are not liberals in the same sense that Franklin Roosevelt and John Kennedy were liberals. Modern populism retains its origin in emotion, in anger that conditions in this country are what they are. Without their knowing it, the modern populists are true radicals in that their formula for action by government presages a true revolution. Modern populists are radical simply because they would root out America's time-honored arrangements, dissolve the monopolies, bring the combinations to heel, and render justice under law. They are enemies to the established order in America.

Lyndon Johnson was conducting the presidency with great success and high personal pleasure in the early summer of 1964, when the political moratorium established by the assassination ran out. After some casting about for a proper title for his presidency, Johnson unveiled the "Great Society" in his commencement address at the University of Michigan in late May. In that speech he opened his campaign for election by his national constituency. As the President described it, the Great Society was to be a place of abundance and liberty for all, a place which holds no poverty or injustice, a place of equality, a place of beauty and creativity, a place in which man can renew his contact with nature. The President concluded, "The Great Society is not a safe harbor . . . It is a challenge constantly renewed, beckoning us toward a destiny where the meaning of our lives matches the marvelous products of our labors. . . ." The Great Society was Johnson's call to rescue America from her sins, her shortcomings, and her proclivity for injustice. At Ann Arbor, Michigan, Lyndon Johnson announced an American millennium.

THE ELECTION OF 1964

The story of the campaign of 1964 is one which has been thoroughly told and almost as thoroughly analyzed. Senator Barry M. Goldwater emulated John Kennedy in his quest for delegate votes, obtained the Republican nomination, and set out to campaign. His campaign was a test of the "hidden vote theory" that most voters are really conservative and that the Republican party had failed to win the presidency in 1960 because it had too long espoused policies put forward by Democrats. Goldwater, an attractive figure and an excellent campaigner, was fully qualified to put the theory to the test. Appropriately, his slogan read, "A Choice, Not an Echo." The 1964 result, for both the theory and Senator Goldwater, was disaster.

The dimensions of Lyndon Johnson's victory in 1964 almost defy comprehension. Since 1824, when the first accurate records were made of popular votes cast in presidential elections, no candidate had previously received the tribute given Lyndon Johnson in 1964. With fewer eligible voters going to the polls than in 1960, Johnson surpassed Kennedy's effort by some 9,000,000 votes, while Goldwater slipped almost 7,000,000 below the Nixon count of 1960. Although Kennedy had defeated Nixon by only two tenths of one percent of votes cast, Johnson polled 61.1 percent in 1964. No mandate of such proportion had ever before been given any President of the United States.

Lyndon Johnson heard this clear call of the voters to lead the nation into the Great Society. With him he carried Democratic candidates for Congress in a sweep not seen since Roosevelt's landslide of 1936. In the Eighty-ninth Congress, Democrats controlled the House 295 to 140 and the Senate 68 to 32. The signs were unmistakably clear. The President had campaigned on the issues; he had described in flowing oratory the goals he had set for the nation and the means to achieve success. He had treated America to the greatest outpouring of frontier radical ideas ever offered on the national scene, and the voters had endorsed his program. His task, as commonly perceived, was to lead the way to the Great Society.

The tone of Johnson's campaign was openly messianic. Performing flawlessly as a modern American Moses, he offered a promised land in which the wealthiest and most productive nation in all human history could at last achieve greatness. The theme, the gestures, the delivery, the very wording of the message came directly from frontier radical politics. The style, later much reviled as "corn pone oratory," achieved a remarkable acceptance by voters throughout the nation. In his own way, probably because of the obvious openness of his campaign, Lyndon Johnson achieved direct discourse with his countrymen.

The theme itself, that Americans had no longer to contemplate the problems of the country, that citizens needed only to roll up their sleeves and set their own houses in order, was a dogma of frontier radicalism which held great political capital in 1964. The task, as delineated by Lyndon Johnson in speech after speech, was to take the wealth of the nation and put it to its most productive uses, to provide every American the opportunity to live in dignity in his own country. The theme, offered and propounded, stated and repeated, pounded home with rural embellishments and stories, or gravely delivered in the cadences of a eulogy for forgotten Americans was impossible to reject. The theme restated the faith espoused by John Winthrop, Thomas Jefferson, Andrew Jackson, William Jennings Bryan, Huey P. Long, and Harry S Truman. The Great Society was the promise to build an earthly paradise in the United States through the people's own labors.

Like Moses, Johnson was not without flaw. He admitted, in frank and open language to crowds in New England, that he had not always supported equal rights for minority groups. But it was in the South, at New Orleans, that Johnson made his most dramatic statement on interracial justice. Looking down the head table at the Jung Hotel toward Senator Russell Long, the President recounted his habit, as a young administrative aide, of going to the floor of the Senate every time Huey P. Long was scheduled to speak. Paying tribute to the elder Long as a man devoted to the people and as a source of Johnson's political philosophy, the President cautioned his fellow Southerners to permit no divisions among themselves, because divisions meant "slow progress toward this better living" for the people of the South. Two thirds of the Democrats and three fourths of the Republicans had voted for the law, and the President had signed it, and he would enforce it. None needed to be told that the law under discussion was the Civil Rights Act of 1964.

Johnson went on to recount the story of an elderly Texas senator who longed to go back to his native state at the end of a long career to "make one more Democratic speech. The poor old state, they haven't heard a Democratic speech in thirty years. All they hear at election time is nigra, nigra, nigra." A gasp of silence greeted the end of the President's remarks and was followed by a slowly building, standing and shouting ovation. The speech, delivered off the cuff and from the heart, was Lyndon Johnson at his best, a truly national leader discussing national policy in the same terms throughout the nation. Here was no "flawed white Southener" caught up in dreams of the old plantation and mint julep and doing "something" for the "darkies"; rather it was Lyndon Johnson, modern populist, moving to undo injustices too long perpetrated against Americans. His radical stand at New Orleans was taken in defense of the Constitution and laws passed by Congress even as it cost him Democratic votes in the South.

From the start of the campaign the President made clear his belief that foreign policy was not an issue. He proposed to follow the Kennedy lead in foreign affairs and rely on two basic factors of conduct: to keep the United States the world's mightiest power and to act reasonably toward both friend and foe. But in a single two-day period of October, three events occurred which shook the international community: Red China successfully detonated her first nuclear bomb; Nikita Khrushchev was deposed by the Soviet Politburo; and Harold Wilson became the Prime Minister of

Britain after thirteen years of Tory control. At almost the same moment, Senator Goldwater indicated that there were things worse than nuclear war, and Johnson proved unable to resist the temptation to attack Goldwater. Assuring the American people that our policies overseas were not endangered by events, the President blasted Goldwater as a "trigger-happy extremist." Clearly, Johnson wanted all the votes of all the people.

A common explanation of the election of 1964 is that Goldwater, an extremist, lost to the candidate of the traditionalist center group of voters. Such a view is not only simplistic but conceals the open espousal of radical programs by President Johnson. In speech after speech the President vowed to increase his war on poverty; he was forthright in his defense of civil rights for all Americans; he demanded improvements in the social security system to include medical care for the elderly; he called for his countrymen to rebuild the cities; he summoned Americans to improve the educational system; and he insisted that citizens and corporations alike must respect the ecology. More than 43,000,000 voters registered approval of the President, who offered to upset most of the nation's long-term social and economic arrangements, agreements, and habits. In November 1964, Lyndon Johnson was the acknowledged folk hero of his country, the Paul Bunyan of American politics. The centrist candidate had won in 1964 only if the center had adopted the new populism.

The voters had responded to the President's call to follow him into the promised land. The campaign was not well organized; schedules were subject to constant change; the President was seldom on time for his appearances; and he was his own campaign manager. With the heat of the summer behind, Johnson's campaign began to gather speed, particularly during a swing through New England in late September. Crowds repeatedly halted the motorcade; the President shook hands and made impromptu speeches; and both old and new New England responded to words and ideas which originated among frontier radicals. The Texas drawl was unmuted when Johnson arrived at Hartford, two hours late and taking forty-five minutes to travel the final five blocks to the speaker's stand to tell his listeners:

> *All that America is, and all that you want America to be is challenged today by those who stand on the fringe . . . Responsible people have only one course of conscience, and that is to choose their country's interest over all other interests.*

The New England region gave Johnson his greatest sweep, Maine with 68.8 percent of the vote and Vermont with 66.3 percent. Connecticut favored the President with 67.8 percent; Massachusetts gave him 76.2 percent; and Rhode Island provided 80.9 percent of its votes to Johnson. In the old Republican strongholds between the mountains, where populism held sway in the 1890s, Johnson shifted the farmers into the Democratic totals to an astonishing degree. Only the white voters of the South, acting out of fear of the Negro and whipped to frenzy by their leaders, denied their votes to Johnson. The poor, the elderly, city dwellers, suburbanites, minority voters, the young—all signed on for the struggle to build the Great Society.

CONSENSUS POLITICS

Within a few months of his accession to the presidency Lyndon Johnson was, as we have seen, achieving legislative victories long denied to President Kennedy. Johnson's combination of knowledge of Congress and its members, the aura of martyrdom which marked the dead President, and Johnson's unique ability to persuade gave new meaning to an old term. "Consensus politics," as the journalists and historians used it from 1963 to 1969, was transformed from its older suggestion of broker government—with the full pejorative meaning—to a new definition of active government at work with the support of most citizens. Before long, President Johnson was caught up in the new terminology as a means to explain his ambivalence toward various interest groups. His personal tendency was a willingness to serve all interests but to become enslaved by none.

"Consensus" also suggested to Lyndon Johnson the theme of gaining affection from individuals and groups on the basis of having helped them. To the Congress he would say, "This has been my home." To businessmen he spoke of government's help to "promote and finance your sales to markets abroad." To the Consumer Assembly the words became, "This is a consumer's administration." For the elderly came the message, "We have taken the bitter years . . . and made them into better years." To the people of underdeveloped regions came the promise, "We will not permit any part of this country to be a prison where hopes are crushed." Finally in 1968, the President defined consensus in his own way, less than twenty-four hours after he had announced his decision to retire from the presidency:

> Sometimes I have been called a seeker of "consensus"—more often in criticism than in praise. And I have never denied it. Because to heal and to build in support of something worthy is, I believe, a noble task.

Such was the consensus that Johnson sought in 1965 following his electoral triumph. To his congressional liaison men Johnson remarked, "I've never seen a Congress that didn't eventually take the measure of the President it was dealing with." The cabinet and White House staff became less Kennedy's and more Johnson's as the President prepared to unveil the Great Society. Even before he delivered his State of the Union address, which detailed his legislative proposals, he remarked to his Vice-President–elect, "Hubert, I figure we have got about nine months to get our way in Congress, no more." In those nine months following January 1965, Congress labored under Johnson's tireless whip to enact the programs needed to establish the Great Society.

Before Congress eventually defeated a major bill designed as part of the Great Society it had passed medicare; the education bill; massive aid to impoverished Appalachia; excise tax reductions of over $4,500,000,000; a law creating the Administration on Aging; a housing act providing for rent supplements for the poor; the Economic Development Act to encourage regional cooperation; the establishment of the new Department of Housing and Urban Development; the National Foundation for the Arts and Humanities; the High Speed Ground Transportation Act; the Water Quality Act; reform of discriminatory portions of the immigration laws; legislation establishing regional medical centers to direct an attack on cancer, heart disease, and strokes; and a law to diminish air pollution. Then on September 29, the House defeated Johnson's proposal for home rule in the District of Columbia.

The President's theory of his relations with Congress has a certain superficial quality of prophecy about it, but he was incorrect. He misjudged badly the strength of his mandate among the American people and the persistence of support for his programs by Congress. At the end of nine months there was a revolt in the Eighty-ninth Congress, but it was a brief revolt triggered by the truth of charges that the Congress had become a rubber stamp. The revolt was based, not on hatred of presidential authority, but on the human need of each member of Congress to see himself as a responsible lawmaker. Immediately after its refusal to pass the District of Columbia bill, Congress moved to pass omnibus farm legislation and authorize $2,400,000,000 for higher education. In 1965 Congress approved more than eighty major Johnson proposals and denied him only three times. Most important for the nation, the Eighty-ninth Congress enacted social and economic change unprecedented in American history.

CIVIL RIGHTS

If Johnson mistakenly downgraded the mandate of 1964 in many areas of activity, there was one major question in 1965 in which the President risked all in support of a principle. The first three months of 1965 saw a voter registration drive at Selma, Alabama, a rural center some fifty miles from Montgomery. Although the Civil Rights Act of 1964 desegregated employment opportunities and public accommodations, the law did nothing about the notorious refusal of registrars in the South to enroll qualified Negroes as voters. During consideration of the Civil Rights Act of 1964 it was generally agreed that any attempt to alter the voting patterns in the South would risk the bill's passage. When Martin Luther King began the voter registration drive at Selma, Sheriff James Clark resorted to violent suppression of mass demonstrations, and a Negro boy was fatally shot on February 18.

On March 7, King's march to Montgomery was turned back under an attack of clubs and tear gas by Alabama state troopers. Governor Wallace blamed the entire affair on "outside agitators" and obtained a court order forbidding further marches. On March 9, King turned back from his proposed march on Montgomery in obedience to the court order, but that evening a Unitarian minister from Boston, the Reverend

James Reeb, was beaten to death by segregationist thugs at Selma. Johnson was not happy. He felt that the civil rights advocates were marching at Selma when they should have been lobbying their congressmen, and the President was highly disturbed by a group of demonstrators who staged a sit-in in the east wing of the White House and shouted obscene taunts at the President.

On March 13, a surprisingly cooperative George Wallace called on the President and assured him that federal force was not necessary if the march to Montgomery was authorized by federal court order. Johnson, however, had already made his decision to intervene with full presidential authority. It was a personal decision coming out of Johnson's experiences as well as his views of the duties of government. He was President, and he would put an end to the old arrangement in the South. At a joint session of the House and Senate on the evening of March 15, Johnson attacked the "crippling legacy of bigotry and injustice." He insisted that "this great, rich, restless country can offer opportunity and education and hope to all—all black and white, all North and South, sharecropper and city dweller." He named the enemies of the people—poverty, ignorance, and disease—and he pledged to attack them. He then intoned the words of the Negro Revolution and left no doubt that he would see to it that Americans everywhere could vote unafraid. "We shall overcome," said the President, and he insured passage of the Voting Rights Act of 1965, by which the President of the United States could protect every citizen in his right to vote.

JOHNSON'S CREDIBILITY GAP

Even as Lyndon Johnson was obtaining revolutionary legislation from Congress and making use of his mandate to create the Great Society, the normal tensions between the

President and the press escalated sharply. In the White House there was concern for the projected personality of the President and for the press descriptions of memories of the Senate Majority Leader as a "wheeler and dealer." Among the journalists there were those who found themselves receiving calls without warning from the White House staff. On occasion the President phoned a journalist to praise a particular column or story but more often to criticize. Before long the press was referring to Johnson's "credibility gap" and implying that the President was telling less than the whole truth.

Every President has had a "credibility gap," but the clash of personalities between Johnson and the press exacerbated Johnson's. The President eventually took the position that he was above being questioned, and the press staked out its claim to be above error and ignorance. The press issued a flood of print in defense of freedom of the press that closely paralleled the concise constitutional logic which the National Rifle Association constantly employs in its defense of the right of every man, woman, and child to own a gun. Both the President and the press assumed godlike stances without any reasonable foundation. The President was advised to "clean up his image," and a whole crew of "credibility gap" warriors appeared. For some of the latter, Johnson's retirement from politics was similar to the blow which Hitler's death dealt to the fortunes of Walter Winchell. Most of the White House press had yet to discover the inestimable rewards of reporting the Vietnam War from Washington, D.C.

In the last week of April 1965, while medicare was being passed in Congress and the voting rights bill had just been enacted, the President was confronted, without warning, by a crisis in Santo Domingo. The Dominican Republic, following the assassination of Dictator Rafael Trujillo in 1961 and a succession of provisional governments, had finally elected a liberal government under Juan Bosch in December 1962.

Bosch was overthrown after seven months by corrupt elements in the military and the oligarchy, which were threatened by his reforms. Bosch's successor, Donald Reid Cabral, was a progressive member of the oligarchy who attempted to build a democratic political system and improve the country's economy. Cabral's reforms received some support from the United States, but Dominican special interests were becoming increasingly restless with Cabral. United States Ambassador W. Tapley Bennett returned to the United States for a short vacation, and pro-Bosch army officers attempted a coup. Within a few hours a civil war broke out in Santo Domingo.

Bennett returned immediately to the Dominican Republic and conferred with his staff. The "country team" reported that the pro-Bosch officers were cooperating with leftist elements, and the ambassador recommended the immediate landing of United States Marines. The President was impressed by the fact that Bennett, his deputy, the three military attachés, and the economic attaché all warned "that American lives are in danger." Bennett was convinced that the pro-Bosch group had been infiltrated by Communists. On April 28, when Johnson was meeting on Vietnam with Rusk, McNamara, Undersecretary of State George Ball, and National Security Advisor McGeorge Bundy, the Bennett message was sent to the White House. The opinion of the President and his advisers was unanimous. The Marines were ordered to land.

Bennett, it was later evident, had exaggerated the extent of Communist influence, and actual involvement of Communists finally became a numbers game. The President first announced the Marine landing as a protection of American lives but failed to notify the Organization of American States of his action. Johnson also decided to include a reference to the protection of "democratic institutions" in his television broadcast after conferring with the leaders of Congress, but Stevenson succeeded in getting the decision reversed. Johnson was, of course, a prisoner of events which he could not control. The alternative of refusing to intervene was never a reality. Had Johnson not intervened and had the Dominican Republic followed the example of Cuba, the military defense of the United States would have been weakened. The President had to act immediately, and he did.

As Bennett's error of judgment became clear and when the Latin American members of OAS realized that they had been rudely treated during this first intervention in the hemisphere since 1925 by American troops, Johnson's diplomatic reputation suffered. Latin American feelings were soothed in sufficient time, and the intervention did bring about conditions conducive to a settlement in Santo Domingo, but the affair triggered the first major outbreak against the leadership of Lyndon Johnson. The attack, more properly a guerrilla war, originated not with conservatives or systems of private political power which had suffered the effects of Great Society legislation but with the liberals. The President became the target of the New York *Times,* the Washington *Post,* the New York *Herald Tribune,* the *New Leader,* and the *New Republic.* The tone of the editorials and articles was shrill and harsh, the wording argumentative. Santo Domingo was just such an occasion which permitted the President to be taken under fire by the liberals.

Liberals had cause to be unhappy with Lyndon Johnson. In earlier days they had felt his lash as Senate Majority Leader, just as congressional liberals were continuing to feel the pressure from the White House. Lyndon Johnson failed to consult with the liberals and their leaders. Secondly, the President was passing through Congress a program which was radical beyond the dreams of most liberal reformers, and the liberals were being transformed into ordinary wheelhorses of the Great Society. Lyndon Johnson was beginning to make the liberal leaders superfluous to the political system, refusing to consult the liberal oracles and merely giving orders to the acknowledged liberal political leaders. To these reasons many a liberal added another—Lyndon Johnson was not a likable person. But the power of the liberals to do more than criticize came into serious question in 1966, when Johnson suffered only the normal off-year losses in Congress: four seats in the Senate and forty-eight in the House. If the liberals were abnormally discontented, the voters were not.

DOMESTIC VIOLENCE AND DISCONTENT

Two conditions troubled Lyndon Johnson's contentment with his work—the slowness of his programs to take hold and the inability of the nation to solve racial differences by legislation. Discrimination, made illegal by Kennedy, Johnson, and moderate Negro leaders, still persisted. Worse for Johnson, his efforts to help minorities were translated into opposition from the white majority. Black extremists gave material aid to incipient racism in the nation by counseling riot, destruction, revolution, and separatism of Negro from white. Extremist leaders felt that Johnson would hesitate to repress minority rioters bent on bettering their lot in life. In this they were right but wrong in their belief that violence could provide positive gains. What violent action did provide was not advancement for the Negro but a new racism where it had not been so obvious before. It rose among residents of the inner cities, the lower classes, poor whites, ethnic groups threatened by neighborhood integration, and the elderly who were too often the target of assault and robbery by young thugs.

By mid 1966 the feeling of rising expectations spread from minority groups to other portions of the population. Writers and artists, movie-makers, self-conscious and self-appointed intellectuals, and members of various youth groups seized upon the methods of the Negro Revolution. To peaceful demonstrations they added acts closely identified with black extremists, riots, arson, and throwing garbage in the streets or "trashing," as it was known. In politics dissidents underwent a sudden discovery of "the Establishment" and spoke of the "new politics," while "new Left" radicals in the universities sought a return to the principles of the pre–World War I anarchists. Taking advantage of liberal Supreme Court decisions regarding censorship, many authors, artists, composers, and film-makers successfully "trashed" the arts. The universities, too often failing in their proper role as seekers and protectors of truth and knowledge, tolerated and condoned puerile acts of violence and destruction by self-delegated student leaders.

By the end of 1967, violence had become an established pattern. That year set a record of fifty major riots, eighty-nine deaths, and destruction of $750,000,000 worth of property. The assassination of Martin Luther King, moderate leader of the Negro crusade, occurred at Memphis on April 4, 1968, and brought riots to that city, Washington, D.C., New York, and a dozen smaller cities. Two months later, Robert F. Kennedy was shot down at Los Angeles as he campaigned for the presidency. Ironically, the death of the younger Kennedy turned the thoughts of many Americans toward forceful repression of violence.

THE WAR IN VIETNAM

An additional blow to those who worked to achieve the Great Society was delivered from Indochina. Almost every evening of 1967 and 1968, the public saw on television intimate details of the "managed violence" of the Indochina war. As never before the American people became familiar with the cruelty and waste inherent in war-making. The effect of this newfound knowledge was magnified by the increasing activities and noise of the "peace group," a strange coalition of sincere pacifists, draft-dodgers, military analysts, and political opportunists. As 1967 came to a close, increasing numbers of people began to speak of America as a "sick society," blithely unaware that their diagnosis thrust all the blame on society and absolved the individual of responsibility. As such, it condoned every act, no matter how idiotic.

Lyndon Johnson's Vietnam policy retained continuity with that of John F. Kennedy. Like Kennedy, the President hoped to aid the government of South Vietnam to retain its sovereignty and beat back the efforts of both the Vietcong and the North Vietnamese. In the winter of 1964–1965, when a series of coups hit the regime in South Vietnam, Johnson rejected escalation of American efforts and insisted on reform of the Saigon government. But Vietcong attacks on American advisers at Pleiku and Quinhon led to American deaths and a systematic bombing of North Vietnam in retaliation. By March 1965, the Saigon government stood in danger of immediate collapse brought on by repeated coups, corruption among its leaders, and heavy desertions of its troops. The President theoretically had a choice of decisions: to use nuclear weapons or to withdraw immediately. Practically, he had no choice except to commit American troops. Public opinion had foreclosed his other options, but the President was a reluctant warrior.

The President found wide public approval for his original stand in Vietnam. The "peace group" had not yet formed; the public remained ignorant of the fact that wars are conducted against people rather than against governments; and there had been no reverses to American troops. Public support for the war continued to build even as events in Vietnam conspired against Lyndon Johnson. As American aid to Vietnam increased, so did opportunities for local corruption; as numbers of United States troops began to wax, local forces found more excuses to avoid combat; as American commanders learned the unreliability of South Vietnam's army, more operations became exclusively American. Although we had no way to know it then, the Vietnam adventure was a replay of an old script entitled "The Loss of China," starring Chiang Kai-shek, which Harry S Truman had refused to produce.

EVALUATION OF JOHNSON'S PRESIDENCY

How shall we assess Lyndon Baines Johnson as President of the United States? Lyndon Johnson ranks among the great Presidents, challenged only by Harry S Truman as the greatest of this century. As President, Lyndon Johnson was a man of passion, skill, daring, and conviction. He brought to his presidency a peerless preparation in experience and philosophy. His mastery of the presidential authority and the restraint with which he exercised his strength mark him as one of history's most skilled political leaders. His presidency was never the empty flourish of a technician, because Johnson was filled with the visions of populist reform, reform based not on cold intellectual analysis of the needs of the nation but anger over rights and opportunities too long denied to Americans. Johnson possessed the "fire in his belly" which marked the leaders of populism, a fire built on the ancient heritage of equality in America.

Lyndon Johnson seethed with energy and vision. His daring to offer the radical programs of the Great Society to his countrymen in 1964 is exceeded only by his unrelenting pursuit of the reforms he offered. His legislation touched almost every segment of American life, and he showed no fear in delivering frontal attacks on the most sacrosanct centers of injustice in America. He treated with contempt the supposedly overpowering lobby of the American Medical Association; he blasted aside the attempt of the real estate lobby to defeat his open housing laws; he crushed the efforts of segregationists to use the police powers of the states to evade his civil rights acts; and his tread was heavy in the "impassable morass" of aid to both public and private education.

He led the people not as king but as emancipator, lifting the heavy burdens of the poor and the oppressed. He was heavy-handed with his opponents or those who sought mere political gain, but he was filled with compassion for those Americans denied a share in the riches of this country and the opportunity to make full use of their personal talents. Lyndon Johnson's legislation fulfilled the Truman agenda in every respect but one—that of bringing the great corporations to the proper service of the nation. He fought the ancient enemies of mankind—poverty, ignorance, and disease—and if he did not overcome, he left a legacy of legislation equal to the task. Johnson led his people to the promised land, but like Moses, he was destined never to enter the Great Society.

Lyndon Johnson's years in the White House saw a nation fully employed during an unprecedented period of prosperity in the country's history; 5,000,000 Americans received job training, and 8,500,000 new jobs were created. Annual expenditures on social programs exceeded $60,000,000,000 in 1968, and federal agencies moved dramatically where state action had been absent or inadequate. Never before had any government made such a commitment to its people as did the Great Society, yet Lyndon Johnson was almost driven from the White House. When he announced on March 31, 1968, his decision to retire from the presidency, Lyndon Johnson's public approval stood at only 36 percent. His lack of support and his belief that he must retire in the interests of peace in Vietnam forced his decision.

Lyndon Johnson was the victim of a concatenation of events, poor advice, and his own misjudgments. He led the nation into heavy involvement in Vietnam because he was convinced that he must do it to prevent the fall of all Southeast Asia to Communism. Supported by public opinion, he subscribed to the thesis that any breach in the wall of containment of Red China must lead to disaster in Asia. His military advisers failed to tell him otherwise. Indeed, both civilian and military warriors of the Pentagon continued to urge even greater escalations than the President would accept, since American military doctrine presupposes that all military situations are susceptible to solution by weight of metal and ordnance. The very decisiveness which Johnson employed so successfully in driving Congress to do his will he was unable to focus against his military advisers. As early as 1964 there were men knowledgeable in Vietnam affairs who knew the truth: South Vietnam could not be saved from her own corruption, her own lack of will, and her own lack of unity.

Not only did Lyndon Johnson receive ill service from his military assistants, but his domestic experts helped him hardly better. Johnson's consensus-building became almost an obsession after the 1964 victory, and no adviser seems to have cautioned him against it. None dared tell him the ancient wisdom that when you attempt to please everyone, you end up pleasing no one. He was advised on "image creation," told to abandon his frontier style of oratory since it was "undignified," persuaded to replace Remington's sharp eye with non-representational art in the White House. He was counseled to abandon his natural plainness of speech and adopt the role of statesman and orator. Lyndon B. Johnson, farmer and rancher, frontier radical leader, plainspoken Texan, was credible; Lyndon B. Johnson, statesman, garlanded with laurel and attired in a toga, was simply incredible. The press created the credibility gap, but the President aided his opponents by his attempts to improve his public image.

The Vietnam War and domestic violence poisoned the wellsprings of the Great Society by diverting the support the President needed for his programs. The loss of popular support for the Great Society was crucial in producing reaction among the American people to Johnson's demands that they achieve, forthwith, guarantees of the worth, dignity, and individual opportunity for every American. Lyndon Johnson insisted that Americans go forward into the Great Society without even a backward glance at the earlier arrangements, monopolies, and injustices so much a part of American history. His Great Society, forced to cope with the Vietnam War and domestic violence, proved unequal to the task of reforming America's society, economy, and political system quickly enough to avoid the recriminations and blame of soured hopes. Lyndon Johnson radicalized the nation with his vision of utopia, and he fell victim to radicalism he could not control. His was the harvest of unfulfillable demands and overblown hopes, demands and hopes frustrated by war and violence. Perhaps he demanded too much and offered too much to the American people, but he neither earned nor deserved the opprobrium and petty viciousness heaped upon him by his countrymen. Perhaps the American people knew instinctively that Johnson had not failed but that they had failed him, and they sought to shift the blame. The peer of Lyndon B. Johnson will not soon be seen again in the presidency, but the triumph of the principles of the Great Society has not been foreclosed.

NOTES

Death of JFK: The best short account of the assassination and funeral of John F. Kennedy is in Theodore H. White, *The Making of the President 1964* (1965), pp. 13–34. Citations to White's work in this chapter are made to the Signet edition, available as a paperback.

Views of LBJ's Presidency: Three works offer reliable acounts of the presidency of Lyndon B. Johnson. Rowland Evans and Robert Novak, *Lyndon B. Johnson: The Exercise of Power* (1966), is a balanced account by two experienced Washington, D.C. journalists. Johnson's prepresidential career is detailed on pp. 5–304. Lyndon B. Johnson's *The Vantage Point* (1971) presents selected incidents and problems of his presidency in a philosophic postpresidential mood. It projects little of the passion and excitement of the Johnson years. Eric F. Goldman, *The Tragedy of Lyndon Johnson* (1968, 1969), is a mix of memoir and history which is flawed by parochialisms of the East Coast and an enduring confusion regarding Texas.

Presidential Speeches: The speech of November 27, 1963 and all subsequent speeches of Lyndon Johnson as President appear in *The Weekly Compilation of Presidential Documents*, continuous publication.

LBJ and Congress: Louis W. Koenig, *The Chief Executive* (revised edition, 1968), pp. 126–127, contains an excellent short analysis of Johnson's relations with Congress in 1965.

The "New Economics": See *The Vantage Point*, pp. 35–37, and *Lyndon B. Johnson: The Exercise of Power*, pp. 368–372.

Populists: Johnson's populist ideas were so thoroughly ingrained that he seldom questioned the origin of his impulses. On only one occasion in *The Vantage Point*, p. 72, does he refer to himself as "this populist politician," but his entire discussion of the War on Poverty, Chapter 4, is phrased in populist rhetoric. The best scholarship concerning Long is T. Harry Williams, *Huey Long* (1969).

New Orleans Speech: The New Orleans speech is related in *The Making of the President 1964*, p. 432, and *The Tragedy of Lyndon Johnson*, pp. 245–248. Johnson, in *The Vantage Point*, pp. 108–110, reports the speech as an attempt to prevent division of the Democrats by the racial issue.

Election Returns: The statistics for the 1964 election returns by state are in *The Making of the President 1964*, pp. 452–455.

Consensus Politics: One of the many advisers urging "consensus politics" on Johnson was Goldman. See *The Tragedy of Lyndon Johnson*, pp. 51–56. For a clear statement of revulsion against a "broker" as President, see John F. Kennedy's statement in *The Congressional Record*, Eighty-sixth Congress, Second Session (January 18, 1960), A353. Tom Wicker, *JFK and LBJ* (1968), p. 205, dates the wreckage of the consensus on November 24, 1963, when Johnson ordered Ambassador Lodge to return to Saigon with a pledge of support for General Duong Van Minh's regime.

Voting Rights: *Lyndon B. Johnson: The Exercise of Power*, pp. 493–497, is a short summary of events at Selma and the President's reaction. *The Tragedy of Lyndon Johnson*, pp. 365–394, is a detailed study of Johnson's role in passage of the Voting Rights Act.

Credibility Gap: On Johnson's credibility gap, see *The Tragedy of Lyndon Johnson*, pp. 409–417. The joke related by Goldman is an old Texas chestnut concerning a judge finding a defendant guilty of perjury.

Crisis in Santo Domingo: Evans and Novak, *Lyndon B. Johnson: The Exercise of Power*, pp. 510–528, provide an excellent distillation of the problems and intervention in the Dominican Republic and agree with Johnson's statements in *The Vantage Point*, pp. 187–205. Goldman's account, pp. 394–398 of *The Tragedy of Lyndon Johnson*, does not jibe with Johnson or Evans and Novak.

Liberal Attack on LBJ: For the liberal attack, see *Lyndon B. Johnson: The Exercise of Power*, pp. 519–529. Goldman, in *The Tragedy of Lyndon Johnson,* devotes a full chapter, "The President and the Intellectuals," to the problem. Johnson displays no rancor except to state his concern for "the irrationality that was besieging our nation and the world," *The Vantage Point,* p. 543.

Vietnam: Johnson, in *The Vantage Point,* p. 529, expresses regret that he could not achieve "a just, and honorable, and a lasting peace in Vietnam." He felt, however, that prospects were better in January 1969 than at any previous time.

Poverty and the Middle Class: Johnson, *The Vantage Point,* pp. 70–87, defines his chief role as champion for the 35,000,000 poor in America, a number which was reduced by 36 percent between 1965 and 1969. Presidential assistant Horace Busby accurately predicted the opposition of the middle class to Johnson's program as the "foe of Negro rights, foreign aid, etc., because . . . they feel forgotten," *The Vantage Point,* p. 71.

South Vietnamese Government: Undersecretary of State George W. Ball, on November 24, 1964, offered a policy study to be used in the event of the collapse of the government of South Vietnam. See Neil Sheehan, *The Pentagon Papers,* published by the New York *Times* (1971), pp. 325–326.

Summary: Johnson summarized his feelings about his presidency in *The Vantage Point,* p. 566: "When we made mistakes, I believe we erred because we tried to do too much too soon, and never because we walked away from challenge."

6. *Richard M. Nixon: The New American Revolution*

Between the last week of October 1964 and the second week of August 1968, Richard M. Nixon performed a political miracle unparalleled in American history. Rising from the depths of his narrow defeat in 1960 by John F. Kennedy and from his political nadir in losing the governorship of California to Edmund (Pat) Brown in 1962, the same Richard Nixon stood before the Republican convention of 1968 to accept his party's nomination for the presidency of the United States. During the three years following Barry Goldwater's monumental defeat in 1964, Nixon had effectively put himself forward as the titular head of the Republican party. By consummate maneuver he eliminated his opponents for the nomination with such success that he was chosen on the first ballot of the Republican convention of 1968. Richard M. Nixon had achieved political resurrection, and he had a single man to whom he owed a debt of gratitude. That man was Richard Nixon. The convention's only real surprise was the choice of Governor Spiro T. Agnew of Maryland, a Rockefeller supporter, as the candidate for Vice-President.

THE ELECTION OF 1968

Richard Nixon's acceptance speech of 1968 fell far short of his performance in 1960. Conceivably he held fewer hopes in 1968, or perhaps it was that so much of the later message was familiar. The speech was directed to "the forgotten Americans, the nonshouters, the nondemonstrators," who constituted the "decent people of America." He intoned that freedom from civil and domestic violence is "the first civil right of every American," but also mentioned that Americans should "build bridges to human dignity across the gulf that separates black America from white America." Finally, as the climax to a short autobiography came the words, "You can see why I believe so deeply in the American Dream." The Republican candidate came away from Miami the beneficiary of a smoothly functioning convention which boosted his personal popularity to a new high.

Nixon also gained from the highly adverse publicity generated by the Democrats three weeks later at their Chicago convention. The party met under the shadows of tragedy and assassination; deep splits were evident in civil rights issues and war policy; and the vocal gymnastics of "instant" leaders seeking national television exposure were frenetic. Lyndon Johnson was the embarrassed and wholly discredited ghost of the Chicago gathering. Self-identified revolutionaries, intent on baiting the police, came to Chicago; "youth leaders," few of them under forty years of age, came to Chicago; hawks, few of them subject to the military draft, and doves, almost all liable to military service, came to Chicago; black separatists, few of whom could survive in a primitive society, along with white supremacists who seemed anxious to return to the antebellum South in their air-conditioned Cadillacs, came to Chicago. The party organization men, the most stable element in the party, also came to Chicago but proved unable to curb the bitterness which erupted inside the convention following reports of violence outside.

The only candidate of national stature considered by the convention was Hubert Humphrey, early civil rights activist, leader of the "young Turks" in the 1948 convention, midwestern liberal, Senate man. To his great personal misfortune, he had served as Vice-President during Lyndon Johnson's descent into his political Hades. If Richard Nixon had arranged his own political resurrection, Humphrey was a political Lazarus, nominated on the first ballot by Johnson's organization men. The antiwar forces, joined by moderates who saw the Vietnam policy as an albatross which Humphrey had to shed to gain election, proposed a platform plank calling for an immediate halt to the bombing of North Vietnam and the opening of serious negotiations. Johnson's organization men, in control of the convention machinery, exerted pressure on Humphrey. Humphrey wilted, embraced the administration stance on Vietnam, and was forced to remain uncommitted on the war until three weeks before the election. Humphrey was freed only when Lyndon Johnson adopted the substance of the antiwar plank as national policy.

Even before the Democratic debacle, Nixon, reflecting on the way he had achieved nomination, adopted a campaign strategy. It was to create a "game plan," implement it with dispatch, monitor its success at set intervals, and stay with "the plan." During September and October, as Nixon moved seemingly without effort toward his goal, Hubert Humphrey barely survived. He became the target of an aroused youth movement at the exact moment that older voters assessed him as too eager to advance the fortunes of America's minorities. With less than forty days left in the campaign, Nixon was far in the lead. The game plan called for him to ride to victory on the wave of anti-Johnson feeling, antiwar sentiment, anti-youth emotionalism, and anti–civil rights fear. Humphrey's assignment was far more difficult, but it came into sharp focus by late September: he had to reunite the Democratic party on the issues or lose the presidency. Humphrey failed because Richard Nixon successfully evaded the issues.

When the votes were counted, Richard Nixon had gained election. Humphrey had achieved remarkable success in reuniting his fragmented party in spite of the loss of the South to Nixon and Governor George Wallace of Alabama. Organized labor's campaign among workers and northern urban Democrats had taken hold, and disenchantment with Wallace set in. When Humphrey sprang to the attack with renewed vigor, the Democrats began to come home. Richard Nixon won election over Humphrey by less than 500,000 votes. The relatively small turnout of voters benefited Nixon. In the large urban centers of Democratic strength in the North, voting dropped dramatically from 9,300,000 in 1964 to only 8,100,000 in 1968, a reduction more than twice the size of Nixon's margin of victory. In 1968 Richard Nixon fell more than 3,000,000 votes behind his performance against John Kennedy in 1960. The new President would be a minority incumbent, having polled only 43.4 percent of the votes, and for the first time since the election of Zachary Taylor in 1849, a new President would begin his first term without a supporting majority of his own party in either house of Congress.

NIXON'S NEW AMERICAN REVOLUTION

Richard M. Nixon's inaugural address was calm, positive, and filled with hope. The President saw the American people beset by "a crisis of the spirit" which prevented solutions to national problems.

> *To lower our voices would be a simple thing . . . We cannot learn from one another until we stop shouting at one another—until we speak quietly enough that our words can be heard as well as our voices. When we listen to "the better angels of our nature," we find that they celebrate the simple things, and the basic things— such as goodness, decency, love, kindness.*

The nation seemed again in good hands.

After more than a month's deliberation, Richard Nixon announced a cabinet carefully selected to support his plans for national leadership. The inclusion of John Mitchell, Robert Finch, and William Rogers gave the President-elect men of long personal friendship on whom he could rely. Bestowing cabinet posts on three governors, Hickel, Romney, and Volpe, indicated Nixon's emphasis on the new role to be played by the states. His choices of Maurice Stans, George P. Schultz, Paul McCracken, and Arthur Burns for important economic and monetary agencies presented an unmistakable aura of "fiscal integrity." The designated Secretary of Defense, Melvin Laird, was a congressman long known to be expert in military and defense matters.

The cabinet was slightly conservative, but it contained no reactionaries or political hacks. It was exactly the right combination to project the image essential to the plan for administering affairs of state—an image of competence, great experience and accomplishment, and the ability to function under the active leadership of Richard Nixon. The new President would be neither king, nor regent, nor proprietor. In keeping with his assessment of the modern American nation and its needs, Richard Nixon would become Manager-in-Chief.

The thrust of the Nixon administration, once under way, revealed that the game plan had little to do with the theme of the inaugural address. Richard Nixon conceived a "New American Revolution," designed to reverse the political trends set in motion by Truman's Fair Deal. Four broad elements, none of them precisely explained, made up the plan. Foreign commitments would be reduced, including a winding down of the Vietnam War; the prestige and powers of state and local governments would be enhanced by an overhaul of the national political structure; the liberal character of the Supreme Court would be redirected toward conservative decisions; and the federal apparatus and bureaucracy would be reorganized to cut costs and decentralize functions. The New American Revolution would be directed by the Manager-in-Chief, assisted by his management team.

All issues became subsidiary to the game plan. The Vietnam War became a part of reversing the mistakes of past generations in foreign policy. High levels of racial tension received similar treatment. The new administration recognized that much of the public disapproval of Lyndon Johnson had been rooted in the collision of rising Negro expectations with increasing fears among whites that racial integration was proceeding too rapidly. Nixon's civil rights adviser, Daniel Moynihan, proposed a period of lessened emphasis on federal help to minorities. His hope was that majority fears would lessen as legislation of the Great Society moved to alleviate the problems of minority groups. Moynihan's term, "benign neglect," was an unfortunate attempt at phrase-making which leaked to the press. Negroes and other nonwhites developed a deeper mistrust of Richard Nixon.

Urban blight and decay posed a political and economic quandary for the New American Revolution, and the attempted solution had two parts: the family assistance plan and revenue-sharing. In place of the elaborate urban welfare plans of the New Frontier and the Great Society, Moynihan proposed use of federal money to create a floor of minimum incomes for welfare recipients—the family assistance plan. The other portion was a proposal to share with the states and local governments the revenues generated by the federal tax structure. Both plans failed to pass the scrutiny of Congress. Welfare reform was not supported, since it would add to the welfare rolls (at least temporarily); and revenue-sharing was not initially approved because Congressman Wilbur Mills, powerful chairman of the House Ways and Means Committee, opposed it. Revenue-sharing was eventually enacted in 1972, an election year for both President and Congress.

The scaling down of funds for urban and welfare programs dovetailed with the new administration's monetary and fiscal plans. Analysis by the President's monetary advisers of the price inflation which began in the last months of the Johnson administration suggested a remedy. Assuming that price inflation was produced solely by federal deficit spending, it would be simple to cut expenditures, look to increased revenues generated by national economic growth, and plan a roughly balanced budget for fiscal 1970. The analysis, which stood Lord Keynes on his head, advocated cutting spending in 1970 and bringing price inflation under complete control in 1971. Surplus federal revenues, to be used for revenue-sharing, would result. Unfortunately for Richard Nixon's policy, most of the inflation was a "cost-push," based on the popular belief that the Democratic prosperity of the past ninety months was vulnerable to Nixon's economies in spending. Prices continued to climb throughout 1969 and 1970.

FOREIGN POLICY COUPS, DOMESTIC PROBLEMS

As the nation prepared for the elections of 1970, Richard Nixon could point to partial success in "winding down" the war in Vietnam. Troop strength in South Vietnam was down to about 365,000 from a high of almost 600,000. The decision to invade Cambodia to reduce enemy supply depots was also heralded as an aid to ending the war. But Asian policy initiatives were countered by serious reverses in the domestic economy. Sharp cuts in space and defense spending created joblessness exceeding 10 percent in areas including and connected to the aerospace industry. Lack of employment among young, poor, unskilled, and nonwhite Americans far exceeded the national average of 6 percent in 1970. This high unemployment rate, contrasted with 3.4 percent in 1968, also included large numbers of middle managers, engineers, and highly trained scientists. In spite of high unemployment and spending cuts by the administration, prices soared 18 percent above 1967 levels, and a greater cost-push was freely predicted by economists and politicians alike.

Both Democrats and Republicans professed to see the elections of 1970 as a national referendum testing the New American Revolution. If the 1970 elections were in fact a referendum, they proved only that the voters were confused. When the results were tallied, the Republicans had gained two seats in the Senate but failed to achieve control. In the House, Democrats added nine seats to tighten their grip. On the state level, the President had campaigned in twenty-one states where Senate seats or governorships were at stake. Of the thirty-six contests in which he intervened, Republicans were elected in thirteen. Some liberals won, others lost. Some conservatives lost, others won. Voter confusion, personalities, and local issues eclipsed the "national referendum" of 1970.

The Ninety-first Congress, whose tenure ended in January of 1971, continued the resistance to executive leadership begun by its predecessor. Noncontroversial portions of the Nixon program were passed: the draft lottery, crime legislation for the District of Columbia, laws against drug abuse, and federal authority to reform mass transit. The President signed Democratic legislation limiting cigarette advertising, providing voting rights for eighteen-year-olds, regulating water pollution, and increasing salaries of federal civilian and military employees. Congress also administered stinging defeats to Richard Nixon by twice rejecting his appointees to the Supreme Court. Neither welfare reform nor revenue-sharing proposals made their way out of committee.

The President's spending priorities also went awry. Congress sharply increased funds requested for improvement of medical facilities, and the legislation drew a veto. On June 30, 1970, the veto was overridden; this was the first time that Congress passed an act over a veto in a decade. Administration proposals to aid education appeared too anemic to the Democratic leadership in Congress, and funds totaling $4,400,000,000 were authorized. Again the President's veto was overridden. In a further legislative defeat, the President was forced to accept stand-by powers to impose a wage-price freeze when the Patman Amendment to the Defense Production Act of 1970 was adopted. Richard Nixon retaliated by impounding and refusing to spend monies above his recommended levels, but he was eventually forced to use the wage-price freeze powers.

By January 1971, the President was ready to alter his economic plan. His budget message, which forecast the first planned deficit ever recommended by a Republican President, called for spending almost $230,000,000,000 in fiscal 1972. The message urged adoption of the "full employment budget," which the President explained as a "self-fulfilling prophecy . . . By operating as if we were at full employment, we will bring about full employment." Vowing to avoid wage and price controls "which would substitute new, growing, and more vexatious problems for the problems of inflation," the President stated his goal: "full prosperity without war, full prosperity without inflation."

The Ninety-second Congress showed little willingness to go beyond the Ninety-first in cooperation with the White House. Hearings occupied the early months of 1971, and only routine legislation was approved. In spite of the President's budget message, laws providing funds for the executive departments were slow of passage, and Congress adjourned for the summer recess without taking action on the budget of the

Department of Defense. It also did not act on welfare reform, revenue-sharing, and federal aid to education. Loan guarantees to rescue the Penn Central Railroad from liquidation were grudgingly voted, and Congress, with great reluctance, saved Lockheed Aircraft Corporation from failure. But in spite of heavy White House pressure, Congress refused to provide funds for an American supersonic aircraft.

The President, having revealed his plan for domestic economic success, turned his attention to foreign policy. He continued his troop withdrawals from Vietnam, supported a conference to reduce troop levels in Europe, restated his high expectations for the SALT talks, and authorized exploratory meetings to reduce tensions in and around Berlin. The United States, under Richard Nixon's leadership, also played a skillful role in obtaining a cease-fire in the Middle East.

In May 1971 came the diplomatic bombshell. Richard Nixon said that he had been invited to visit Peking and had agreed to meet with Chou En-lai in February 1972. Clearly implied in the announcement was some level of recognition and United Nations membership for Red China, now known as the Chinese Peoples' Republic. The Japanese ambassador in Washington, D.C. had only ten minutes' warning prior to the announcement. Taiwan and Saigon learned of the major policy revision from the press services. Within a few months the President also announced a state visit to Moscow scheduled for May 1972. In visiting the two prime centers of Communist power, Richard Nixon opened negotiations with America's chief antagonists of a generation. By his dramatic diplomatic reversal he also stirred up serious doubts regarding America's future policy in both Europe and the Pacific. In trading old friends for new, the President assumed the additional risks inherent in his choices.

Early in August 1971, with the China and Soviet overtures still under public discussion, the President learned of domestic economic disaster. The facts were incredible! In the first half of 1971 the nation suffered its first adverse international exchange of merchandise since 1893; by the end of April foreigners held dollar claims of $47,700,000,000, while America's entire gold stock was only $13,500,000,000. Industrial productivity, as measured by the Federal Reserve System, had fallen to only 106 percent of the 1967 average and stood a full 1.4 percent below that of July 1970. The recorded trade deficit of the first half of 1971 actually exceeded all combined trade deficits since 1962.

On Sunday, August 15, 1971, the President addressed the nation and announced his new economic policy. Prices, wages, and rents were frozen for ninety days in the United States, and foreigners could no longer redeem dollars for gold. The dollar would "float" in international exchange markets, and a surtax of 10 percent was placed on all imports. Foreign aid would be cut by $350,000,000 and domestic spending by $4,700,000,000. Although the message was attuned to problems of foreign trade, the domestic economic indicators offered little hope. Price inflation in 1971 stood at a rising 6.6 percent annually, and unemployment gripped over 5,500,000 Americans, 6 percent of the labor force.

When the freeze period ended in November, Richard Nixon adopted Phase Two, designed to solve the problems of inflation, joblessness, and the trade deficit. Phase Two remained in effect until January 1973, when it was replaced by Phase Three. Phase Three relaxed the economic controls of Phase Two on both wages and prices and depended on self-restraint of workers and businessmen for its success. By the middle of June 1973, it was apparent that inflation, particularly in prices of food, was out of hand, and the President announced a new sixty-day freeze, to be replaced later by Phase Four. From the announcement of the 1973 freeze it was obvious that neither Richard Nixon nor any of his economic advisers was able to harness the economy for the well-being of the nation.

THE ELECTION OF 1972

Even before the President's dramatic series of policy initiatives at home and abroad, Democrats began to take a sanguine attitude toward the presidential election of 1972. The Vietnam War had become the Indochina War; the President's economic policies had created what he later called a "recession"; social and urban problems were not being solved; and our foreign trade had become a nightmare. It seemed that every Democrat in the United States Senate was actively seeking the Democratic nomination in 1972. The lack of any great love for Richard Nixon by the American people and the adoption of the McGovern-Fraser rules, which provided a truly open Democratic convention, added to the list of prospective candidates.

Serious contenders included Senator Edmund Muskie of Maine, who had run for the vice-presidency in 1968, and Senator Hubert H. Humphrey of Minnesota, who almost won the prize in 1968. Senator Henry M. Jackson of Washington, defense expert and civil rights champion, was interested, as was Senator Fred Harris of Oklahoma, who called himself a populist. Senator Edward M. Kennedy, the "dream candidate" of many Democrats, stated his disinterest in the nomination, but few believed him. Governor George C. Wallace of Alabama insisted that his loyalty to the party remained unclouded by his actions in 1968. There was also Senator George S. McGovern of South Dakota, who announced his availability on January 17, 1971. All announced candidates agreed to run in various state primaries.

The significant primaries began in New Hampshire on March 7 and ended in California on June 6, 1972. Victory in the California primary gave George McGovern sufficient delegate votes to assure his nomination on the first ballot at Miami on July 17. Four factors propelled McGovern to his convention victory: the new convention rules invited more widespread participation of Democrats than ever before; McGovern had built a dedicated and effective primary organization; he had refused to be disheartened by his permanent low standing in opinion polls; and he appealed to the consciences of his fellow Democrats. He was more evengelist than politician, the decent man rather than the schemer.

The Democratic convention began on July 17, the theory being that the candidates could use the time before Labor Day to campaign against the incumbent. Convention meetings, each running into the early morning hours, were conducted by Chairman Lawrence O'Brien. He presided with careful impartiality and permitted the airing of all shades of opinion. As a direct result, George McGovern made his acceptance speech on Thursday morning at three o'clock. In his address, McGovern charted the dangerous course successfully navigated by John F. Kennedy and brought to full fruition by Lyndon Johnson, an appeal to conscience and idealism. In accepting the nomination, the candidate called upon the nation to turn away from indifference and studied inattention to suffering, corruption, racial and economic discrimination, and the folly of war.

McGovern summoned the traditional virtues of America to aid him in his task as he repeated his theme, "Come home, America." In the best populist tradition, he attacked the corporations, corruption in government, unfair taxes, inequality of economic and social opportunity, and an immoral war. His oration, more a sermon than a political speech, called upon Americans to repent, to put away their lack of concern for their neighbor, and to follow conscience to a new national unity. The speech was in the best tradition of Bryan,

Long, Truman, and Johnson, to which McGovern added the moral fervor of Walter Rauschenbusch's social gospel.

The Republicans came to Miami with their candidate already selected, and their chief task was to attract a large television audience. The convention necessarily took on a format of advertising the candidates and providing entertainment. Each session was flawlessly programmed to show the President in the performance of his duties. Each speaker read from a prepared script while the cameras panned slowly through the delegate sections to disclose Republicans of middle-class grooming and sufficient numbers of properly shorn and attired young people. Even the protesters who came to attack "the establishment" cooperated by providing a few nasty attacks on delegates' buses. The Republicans at Miami displayed an ordered serenity of total planning in contrast to the open and often disorderly democratic process which marked the Democratic convention of 1972.

The Nixon campaigners understood completely the advantages which accrue to an incumbent President. The campaign strategy was simple: Keep the President from discussing any issue which would not redound to his benefit, and avert or minimize any incident which would threaten his re-election. The President would issue radio and television messages in carefully controlled surroundings and rely on "surrogate campaigners" to appeal for "four more years" in which to complete his work. The entire campaign, including Republicans and "Democrats for Nixon" organized by John Connally, would be directed, coordinated, and financed by the Committee to Reelect the President.

The positive thrust of the President's campaign was confined to foreign policy: the quest for "a generation of peace" and "peace with honor" in Indochina. The domestic theme was essentially negative and concentrated on those trends and policies the President opposed. He was against the "welfare ethic," against busing to achieve racial balance in the schools, against drug abuse, against radicalism, against abortion, against draft evaders and military deserters, against crime in the streets. The Republican campaign addressed itself to voters increasingly ambivalent towards high unemployment, decaying cities, poverty, unequal social and economic opportunity, and an economy subject to inflation and inability to compete in world markets.

George McGovern proved himself an amazingly inept campaigner. He frittered away the time before Labor Day in the unhappy and indecisive substitution of R. Sargent Shiver for Senator Thomas Eagleton as his running mate. McGovern also decided to campaign as a "part of the news," only to find that he wasted his efforts in answering charges by minor or local Republicans. His paid political telecasts were far more effective and revealed the candidate as an evangelist fully capable of articulating the populist message. He demanded an end to the Indochina War, heavy cuts in arms expenditures, an end to wage and price controls, jobs for all persons ready to work, and the redistribution of income through tax reform.

The campaign of 1972, billed by President Nixon as "the choice of the century" and by Senator McGovern as "a spiritual experience," proved both expensive and irrelevant. Both counted on the votes of a dissatisfied electorate. In setting himself in opposition to the forces of discontent in the nation, Nixon sought voters who feared the future and wanted reassurance. The Democratic candidate tried to galvanize the discontent into a great machine of change in America. The President counted on apathy, alienation, and a basic desire among voters to halt change and avoid uncertainty. The challenger staked his opportunity on an appeal to conscience re-

sulting in a great outpouring of idealist voters anxious to renew the promise of America. Nixon was right in his analysis,
McGovern wrong.

The landslide vote to reelect President Nixon in 1972
was almost a record. The President's percentage of the popular vote was exceeded only by Lyndon Johnson's in 1964, and
his control of the electoral votes came close to Franklin
Roosevelt's sweep of 1936. Yet voter participation, in terms
of those eligible to vote, fell to its lowest level since 1948,
with less than 55 percent of all eligible voters going to the
polls. Of almost 140,000,000 potential voters in the nation,
only 76,500,000 actually voted. November 7, 1972 marked
a flight from reality by citizens upset by the unlovely face
of America in the 1970s. Many voters stayed home, while
others may have diverted themselves with an imaginary executive order barring the existence of the poor, the uneducated, the criminal, the elderly, and the Negro. Few found
difficulty in singing of America: "Thine alabaster cities gleam/
undimmed by human tears." It was a spectacular but peculiar
mandate for Richard M. Nixon, much of the mandate a direct
result of the remnants of America's "peculiar institution."

The election of 1972 brought Richard Nixon a personal
and electoral triumph based on the voters' weariness and
wariness of the poor, the uneducated, and the Negro. Mc-
Govern reaped the harvest of self-doubt sown by the Indochina War and the inability of the Great Society to immediately fulfill its promise of the better life. McGovern's hope of
a new populist majority fragmented on the rock of fear created
by the racial integration of northern cities and the increasing
entry of minority groups into American social and economic
life. The peculiarity of the Nixon victory was emphasized by
the Republican gain of only thirteen seats in the House of Representatives and the actual net loss of two seats in the Senate
to Democrats. With little hope of Republican control of

Congress to be gained in 1974, Richard Nixon bade fair to become the first President ever to hold the White House for eight years while Congress remained in the hands of his opponents. In 1972 the voters chose to retain the familiar without risking the future; it was a decision to remain stagnant rather than to chance a new course of action.

EVALUATION OF NIXON'S PRESIDENCY

At the close of five years of Richard M. Nixon as President of the United States, how shall we assess him? He must be recognized as a shrewd, self-disciplined, and resilient politician. His political resurrection and his electoral sweep of 1972, unique in the history of the nation, constitute a tribute to Nixon's strength and tenacity. His willingness to "tough it out" in the face of adversity is characteristic of the man. He has not developed into a compelling charismatic figure in the mold of Eisenhower or Kennedy, and he has preferred to set himself apart from the general citizenry. Indeed, his studied attempts to project honesty, openness, and sincerity have often been interpreted as the prefabricated product of the professional image-makers.

Conduct of Office

Nixon's conduct of the presidential office has been characterized by two divergent trends. One is his tendency toward the dramatic, flamboyant gestures of a popular leader; the other is his rather prosaic definition of the presidential task as that of Manager-in-Chief. Richard Nixon has repeatedly demonstrated his capacity for sudden and dramatic acts, especially in foreign policy. In the midst of winding down the Vietnam War, he transformed the combat into the Indochina

War by authorizing a sudden and heavy attack on enemy sanctuaries in Cambodia and Laos. His innovative reversals of policy toward mainland China and the Soviet Union, together with his refusal to terminate the bombing of Cambodia by United States aircraft, demonstrate his self-confidence and will to prevail.

But Nixon's conception of the role of the President in governing the United States is at odds with his taste for the dramatic and unexpected. Even before his inauguration in 1969, as previously noted, he created a management team of competent, efficient, and successful men willing to serve the nation. It was expected that the President, using his cabinet as a management group, would design a game plan to achieve the presidential goals. The early impression was that the eleven executive department heads would be active participants in policy-making. In practice, however, Richard Nixon increasingly modeled himself on the Kennedy and Johnson pattern of allowing the cabinet to fall into disuse. Perhaps he had learned that the cabinet is too large and too heavily burdened to constitute a true management team.

The President soon turned to a small group of White House advisers as his consultants, making little use of cabinet expertise. In foreign policy Richard Nixon has relied heavily on Henry Kissinger; the Department of State was clearly not prepared for the China bombshell. Troops were withdrawn from Vietnam and mainland China's entry into the United Nations was supported, both without comment on future security arrangements in the Pacific. During negotiations leading to the Vietnam cease-fire and the Peking visit of early 1972, Secretary of State William Rogers was openly relegated to a ceremonial role. As a result of summit meetings held in Peking, Moscow, and Washington, D.C., the Department of State has been left to explain policies not of its making.

Richard Nixon preferred to obtain his domestic advice, for the most part, from his White House chief of staff, H. R. Haldeman, and his Domestic Council head, John Erlichman. During John Mitchell's term as Attorney General, he was chief adviser on racial policies, urban unrest, and the radical student movement. In addition, Mitchell reviewed the proposed appointees to the Supreme Court, but in 1972 Mitchell resigned as Attorney General to head the Committee to Reelect the President. The Nixon economic decisions have relied on several counselors, the most durable of them being George Schultz. Paul McCracken, Arthur Burns, Casper Weinberger, and even John Connally have been in the ascendency at various times, but the President has seemed to pay closer heed to Schultz than to other economic analysts.

Yet the abandonment of the cabinet as the chief management team and the substitution of a small number of presidential advisers has not brought undiluted success to the President. Richard Nixon achieved a cease-fire in Vietnam, but his foreign policy initiatives had unpredictable results. The proof of his diplomatic innovation lies in the future conduct of Peking, Moscow, Bonn, Tokyo, and Taiwan. Long-term trade trends in Europe and the Pacific, as well as the future development of NATO and the SALT talks, will provide the cost/benefit data regarding Nixon's dramatic foreign policy. Domestically, racial tensions and urban blight remain as unsolved major problems of the Nixon administration, although civil disturbance and urban riots have decreased to insignificance since Richard Nixon became President in 1969. In economic matters the President has had little success in the fight against inflation and joblessness.

The original Nixon concept of the game plan being changed only when necessary has been retained. In general, it appears that patently unsuccessful strategies have been retained too long. This was the case when the New Economic

Policy failed to check price inflation and unemployment and when the full-employment budget achieved only a portion of its predicted goals. The legislative game plan for dealing with the Democratic Congress—to whipsaw the majority by the use of the veto and impoundment of appropriated funds—was a novel approach. The President could be an activist, moving toward negative goals, only so long as the Congress did not become unified by adversity. By the middle of 1973 is was apparent that the old game plan had become counterproductive relative to success with Congress. Given Richard Nixon's desire to excel as President, together with his personal flexibility and pragmatism, this reluctance to change game plans seems inconsistent with his character.

If we judge game plans as managers do, most of Richard Nixon's domestic game plans have failed. If we are to grade the manager on the basis of goals achieved, the Manager-in-Chief has failed. Much of what a manager can accomplish depends on the information made available to him by his staff and the clarity of the analysis provided. What is so painfully evident in the economic crisis measures which the President adopted after August 15, 1971 is the lack of clear analysis and an agreed game plan to force economic progress. The growing shortages of food and energy, together with on-again, off-again price controls and the obvious casting about for partial solutions, evidence a lack of comprehensive analysis. In foreign policy the indications of *ad hoc* policymaking were clear in the cavalier expulsion of the Taiwan Chinese from the United Nations in spite of the United States' efforts to salvage part of Taiwan's position and in the refusal of NATO allies to take seriously American attempts at continued leadership. President Nixon has been unready to replace those advisers who have failed to provide him the information and analysis he so badly needs. Only future success can vindicate the Nixon advisers and give credibility to

Richard Nixon's concept of the President as Manager-in-Chief.

Judged by the standards of the Truman social agenda, President Nixon has done little to achieve national goals. Nonwhite minorities and the poor have made no significant gains under the Nixon leadership; medical care has been only grudgingly extended to additional elements of society; full employment rates have given way to unacceptable levels of joblessness; public housing has been crippled through reduced expenditures at a time of rising costs; and both aid to education and federal funding of hospital construction have been increased only over the President's veto. In fairness to Richard Nixon, however, it must be stated that he has never endorsed the Truman social agenda. Indeed, as noted above, President Nixon undertook from the start to undo what he saw as the "mistaken" programs of the Fair Deal and the Great Society.

The Nixon presidency must stand or fall solely on the President's ability to obtain popular and congressional acceptance of his plans for managing, conducting, and moving forward the nation's tasks. He is, as David Broder has put it, "a man in search of a constituency." The possible constituency was lost at the same time Richard M. Nixon assumed a unique place in the history of the republic—in the early morning of June 17, 1972. What was eventually revealed was the most serious and corrosive attack ever made upon the Constitution of the United States and the rights of American citizens. Whether its source was a mixture of megalomania and paranoia or simple arrogance tinctured with stupidity makes little difference. The controlling fact is that the Nixon White House contained a powerful group of "true believers" whose garrison-state frame of mind permitted them to justify gross violations of the Constitution, statutory federal law, and simple human decency.

The Watergate Conspiracy

Frank Wills, a security guard at the Watergate office and residential complex in Washington, D.C., summoned the metropolitan police when he noted that door latches had been taped open. The police arrived and arrested five men, all of them employees of the Committee to Reelect the President, in the act of placing electronic surveillance devices in the offices of the Democratic National Committee. The act was passed off as a "prank" or "caper," and lawsuits by the Democrats seeking damages were declared to be simply "playing politics." Watergate had no effect on Richard Nixon's electoral triumph in 1972, since no Democrat, given the President's stands on the issues, could have defeated him. Yet, on April 30, 1973, the President felt compelled to speak out against charges of personal complicity in what had become the Watergate conspiracy.

The events of April 1973 were incredible. The acting director of the Federal Bureau of Investigation was denied Senate confirmation and faced possible criminal indictment; the President's chief legal counsel, John W. Dean III, was identified as a part of the conspiracy; and the burglars, all former employees of the Central Intelligence Agency, were convicted of burglary and conspiracy. One of the Watergate burglars, James McCord, offered further information about the break-in and political espionage in an effort to obtain a lighter prison term. By the end of April, the sordid details of a calculated attack on the American political system began slowly to float to the surface. What became apparent was that the Committee to Reelect the President had contained a criminal conspiracy.

Under such circumstances the President had only two choices of role, those of criminal and dupe. Nixon chose the latter. In his nationally televised speech of April 30, he announced the resignations of Attorney General Richard Kleindienst, Chief of White House Staff H. R. Haldeman, and Domestic Council head John Erlichman. John Dean III was summarily fired. The President explained that he was so busy with presidential duties that he had entrusted the electoral campaign to others. He stated that he had been repeatedly assured that the White House had no connection with the burglary, and he called for punishment of any person who had violated the law. Richard Nixon then announced the appointment of Elliott Richardson as his new Attorney General and charged him with making a full investigation. The President took formal responsibility, but he asked the American people to turn away from Watergate and interest themselves in problems of inflation, equality of opportunity, and foreign policy. Richard Nixon risked all on a single speech, but he failed to salvage his reputation.

In May and June it was learned that the Watergate burglars had earlier broken into the offices of a Los Angeles psychiatrist in an effort to obtain the medical records of Daniel Ellsberg, a defendant in the Pentagon Papers case. Egil Krogh, a former Erlichman assistant, admitted that he had planned and controlled the Los Angeles break. A reelection committee employee, Donald Segretti, was indicted on charges of manufacturing and distributing scurrilous campaign charges on Edmund Muskie stationery. The deputy director of the committee admitted that he had ordered the Watergate break-in to improve devices previously planted in Democratic headquarters. The committee treasurer admitted destroying records of contributors on orders from the head of the Reelection Finance Committee, Maurice Stans. In New York a grand jury indicted Stans, former Secretary of Commerce under Nixon, and John Mitchell, Nixon's former law partner and Attorney General. The charge was conspiracy to "fix" an investigation of a stock swindle after a contribution of $200,000 had been made to the committee. Within a few days the chairman of the Securities Exchange Committee resigned, protesting his innocence.

The United States Senate appointed a select committee, headed by Senator Sam Ervin of North Carolina, to investigate all aspects of the election of 1972. The Senate also initially withheld its consent to the appointment of Richardson as Attorney General. Only after Richardson announced the selection of Harvard Law School professor Archibald Cox as special prosecutor for Watergate did the Senate confirm Richardson. Senator Ervin, a highly respected constitutional lawyer and former North Carolina judge, opened hearings in mid May. By the end of June it was clear that the American political system had undergone an almost fatal assault by the Nixon palace guard. When the Nixon men moved into the White House, they brought with them a cynical view of the uses to which the presidential authority could be put. Under the hypocritical covers of national security and a drive to restore law and order to a restless nation, the President's men had organized a conspiracy against the American people.

The President's appointees had engaged in systematic violations of the law, electronic surveillance of all possible opponents, manufacture and misrepresentation of documents, destruction of evidence, burglary, and misuse of the security agencies of the United States for political purposes. The Constitution of the United States, civil and political rights of American citizens, and the criminal laws of the nation were violated on a continuing and almost casual basis. The Federal Bureau of Investigation and the Central Intelligence Agency, as well as the National Security Council, the Department of State, the Internal Revenue Service, and the Department of Justice itself, were used and coordinated into the plot. The conspirators used their power over the executive branch to frustrate the will of the legislative branch and to try to intimidate or influence the federal judiciary. They subverted the authority of the President, diverted public powers to private use, and filled the higher echelons of the federal government with political thugs. Because of the success of the plot, the Watergate conspiracy is the gravest threat to popular control of government in the history of the Republic. (To pursue this thought, see "Watergate vs. the Constitution" on page 191.)

Even more alien to America than the execution of the plot was the mentality of the plotters themselves. Almost without exception they were well-educated members of the middle class, many of them lawyers. They held no ideology of Left or Right which might impel them to serve a "higher cause." They were driven only by a lust for power, and having achieved untrammeled control of the presidential authority, they sought to perpetuate their hold. The conspirators were not political amateurs. Instead they were amoral managers who conducted their plot toward a managerial end: to substitute their "superior judgment" for that of the American people. In a curious and perverted logic, laws were broken to advance law and order; dissenters were illegally suppressed or spied upon to protect national security; certain political "enemies" were listed, to be treated outside the law; the Federal Bureau of Investigation and the Central Intelligence Agency were unlawfully used to prevent subversion; and illegal listening devices were utilized to protect the nation against people "disloyal" to the President. The conspirators, under cover of the Committee to Reelect the President, hoodwinked thousands of Republican leaders and Democrats for Nixon at the national, state, and local levels in a mockery of the electoral process. The actions of the conspirators, in the light of their fear and renunciation of the traditional American political process, mark them as pariahs in American life.

Less than five years after Richard Nixon became President the Watergate conspiracy claimed its forfeit. The Nixon administration was a shambles. The New American Revolution was dead; the managerial approach to more efficient government had proved fruitless; and the peculiar mandate of 1972 had evanesced. Domestic and foreign policies stood in disarray. At home the hard facts of uncontrolled inflation, persistent unemployment, and shortages of food and energy could not be shrugged off. The Council of Economic Advisers openly predicted the probability of economic recession in 1974. Allies of long standing both in the Pacific and in Europe were disaffected from support of the United States. Japan and Taiwan had been cast aside in haste to court the mainland Chinese. Nixon's policy of detente with the Soviet Union thrust new pressures on the North Atlantic Treaty Organization, and the alliance foundered in the new war which broke out in the Middle East in 1973. A generation of mutual defense agreements between the United States and Europe fell victim to an Arab boycott of oil shipments to nations supporting Israel. Of all NATO allies, only Portugal and the Netherlands stood with America in the face of a Soviet-sponsored attack on Israel in 1973.

More critical to Richard Nixon was his inability to dispel the climate of suspicion of him which engulfed the American people. New and ugly revelations regarding Watergate continued; Vice-President Agnew resigned his office and was convicted of tax fraud; and special prosecutor Archibald Cox was summarily removed by presidential order. Attorney General Elliot Richardson and his deputy, William Ruckleshaus, resigned their posts rather than carry out that order. Even the worldwide military alert ordered by the President in response to the new Middle East crisis was seen by many Americans as a new ploy to divert public attention from Watergate. Congressional confirmation of Congressman Gerald Ford to replace Agnew as Vice-President only revived earlier cries for the President to resign or be impeached. Information released by the White House to refute charges against the President of personal dishonesty disclosed only that he had become a millionaire during his first term of office and that he had paid income taxes equivalent only to those paid by the head of a family of four earning $8,000 per year.

The President reverted to the role of his traditionalist predecessors. Watergate charges and Nixon's personal crisis of public confidence foreclosed policy-making, and the President seemed able to handle matters only on a one-by-one basis. Crises in food production, reduced deliveries of meat to retail markets, and explosive rises in food prices found the President with *ad hoc* remedies hurriedly put forward, seemingly without regard to how the solutions impinged on other problems. There was little evidence that the President foresaw the energy crisis which was sharpened by the Arab oil boycott. Indeed, he reacted ideologically to suggestions of gasoline rationing by his energy "czar," former Governor John Love of Colorado. Love resigned. The administration was riddled by resignations and indictments. Presidential leadership came to a virtual halt as Richard Nixon fell to his minimum effectiveness as President of the United States. Such was the price of the Watergate conspiracy.

The temporary success of the conspiracy, the coordination of the federal apparatus as tools of the plotters, and the self-proclaimed failure of the President to safeguard his authority combine to deliver the verdict on Richard Nixon as President of the United States. His presidency, regardless of what he may accomplish during the remainder of his tenure, will be marked by the Watergate conspiracy and by Richard Nixon's inability to exert the moral leadership essential to the successful conduct of the presidency.

Yet the real tragedy of the Watergate conspiracy inures not to President Nixon, but to the American people. While the Constitution was being violated by public officials, during days when individual rights were being swept away, at a time when political mobsters ranged the White House itself, too many people in and out of government cooperated in the conspiracy. American liberties were not guarded by an eternally vigilant people. Instead, the plot was disclosed and the nation saved by the suspicions of Frank Wills and the fears of James McCord. The Watergate conspiracy became the most peculiar and the most dangerous portion of Richard M. Nixon's peculiar mandate of 1972.

NOTES

Political Resurrection: The political resurrection of Richard M. Nixon is described in vivid detail in Jules Witcover's *The Resurrection of Richard M. Nixon* (1970). Nixon's more fatalistic view in earlier days is in his *Six Crises* (1962). The story of the election of 1968 is well told in Theodore White, *The Making of the President, 1968* (1969). An unusually brilliant analysis of voting behavior and the reasons for the Nixon victory in 1968 appears in Richard M. Scammon and Ben Wattenberg, *The Real Majority* (1970). Kevin Phillips's *The Emerging Republican Majority* (1969) bears an unmistakable flavor of currying favor with the Nixon administration in its dedication and in the questionable statistical techniques employed to demonstrate a permanent Republican majority now abuilding in the nation. Joe McGinniss's *The Selling of the President, 1968* (1969) is an "inside" view of the Nixon television campaign in which McGinniss accepts, with excessive gullibility, the view that candidates can be sold like cereals or detergents.

1968 Election Returns: Nixon gained 43.4 percent of the votes, Humphrey 42.7 percent, and Wallace a surprising 13.5 percent.

Management Team: The concept of the "management team" cabinet was the dominant theme of the postelection period of 1968.

New American Revolution: The New American Revolution, announced in the State of the Union message of 1970, was tied to the goal of reduced federal expenditures through restructuring the federal administration, revenue-sharing with the states, and welfare reform. The administration undertook sharp decreases in defense spending and leveled off nondefense expenditure. The armed forces were cut by 400,000 in 1970, and the Defense Department dropped civilian employment by over 100,000. Employment by primary defense contractors fell some 150,000; and secondary suppliers lost as many jobs. See the *Federal Reserve Bulletin* (December 1970), pp. 871–872.

"Cost-Push" Inflation: "Cost-push" inflation is based in the popular belief that prices will rise rapidly until checked by business recession. The individual or firm attempts to protect against future price inflation by "getting it now" and thus fuels more inflation. This is a sharp contrast to the "demand-pull" inflation after World War II which was rooted in surplus demand coupled with a shortage of goods.

Path of Recent Inflation: Central to the price inflation is the long-term decline in productivity of American industry in relation to investment and labor force. The first resulting balance of payments deficit came at the end of the Eisenhower administration, and the 1962 deficit reached $2,700,000,000. By 1966 the trend had reversed, but the Vietnam War caused a new imbalance of $3,400,000,000 in 1967. Both 1968 and 1969 saw a favorable balance of payments. See the *Federal Reserve Bulletin* (December 1970), pp. A72–A73.

Budget Deficits: The budgetary deficit of the 1971 fiscal year exceeded $20,000,000,000. Total deficits projected for fiscal 1972 and 1973 exceeded $30,000,000,000.

Full Prosperity Budget: The "full prosperity budget" appears in the *Economic Report of the President* (February 2, 1971).

It is a curious reversal of Say's law, expounded by the French nineteenth-century economist J. B. Say.

Trade Deficit: The major portion of the trade deficit was caused by huge imports from Japan. Between 1960 and 1969 imports of Japanese steel rose from $76,000,000 to almost $7,700,000,000. Television receivers from Japan were a negligible import in 1960 but reached a value of almost $250,000,000 in 1969. Automobiles imported from Japan in 1960 cost only $2,000,000 but jumped to $300,000,000 in 1969 and topped $450,000,000 in 1970. See *United States Trade with Japan, 1960–1969* and 1970 *Supplement,* United States–Japan Trade Council (1971). Ray Cromley's syndicated column of September 5, 1971, "Slow Modernization of Industry Complicates Nixon's Economic Plan," lists annual German industrial investment at 19 percent of gross national product, Japanese investment of 29.6 percent of GNP, and United States investment of only 11 percent of GNP.

Economic Crisis of 1971: The most concise statement of the 1971 crisis is in *Time,* August 23, 1971. By June 1973, when the President announced a new freeze, prices were rising at a rate of 7.2 percent, and food prices had jumped a full 15 percent in the previous year. The federal deficit for fiscal 1973 was about $18,000,000,000, but the unemployment rate had slowed to about 5.5 percent. Proposed for fiscal 1974 was a budget of $268,700,000,000 and a deficit of $12,700,000,000. When Phase Four was announced on July 17, 1973, it was the fourth plan attempted in the twenty-three months after the crisis of 1971.

1972 Campaign and Election: The campaign proved irrelevant, since the portion of votes cast for President Nixon and Senator McGovern closely approximated the findings of the national opinion polls taken prior to the onset of the campaign. Nixon obtained 60.9 percent of the votes, slightly less than Johnson's 61.6 percent in 1964. The President gained 520 electoral votes, just short of Roosevelt's 523 in 1936. The Bureau of the Census estimated the turnout of voters at only 54.8 percent of potential voters, lowest since 1948.

Isolation of Nixon: Richard Nixon's desire to isolate himself from most Americans was a matter of choice which later proved costly.

Price Inflation: The Department of Labor's Consumer Price Index indicated that prices in June 1973 stood at 132.4 percent of prices in June 1967. Most of the price inflation has occurred since 1969. In 1973 prices rose by 8.8 percent.

Ramifications of Policy Changes: Richard Nixon has not failed to produce "grand designs" of policy, both domestic and foreign. Yet, there is a perplexing lack of adequate staff work and specific forecasting of the consequences of changed policy. The results of the China overture, the Soviet grain deal, and the agreement to participate in the Soviet-initiated European Security Conference at Helsinki were definitely calculable. On all these occasions involving major policy decisions, no cost-benefit study appears to have been made.

   During the summer of 1973 William Rogers resigned as Secretary of State. Henry Kissinger was appointed by the President to replace Rogers and was confirmed by the Senate on September 21, 1973. Kissinger continued as assistant to the President for national security affairs.

Watergate vs. the Constitution: In assessing the importance of the Watergate conspiracy, we must consider the nature of that attack on the Constitution in relation to the military attack of the Confederacy during the American Civil War. What was at issue between 1861 and 1865 was the permanence of the Union, and the Constitution of the Confederate States of America, except in the case of slavery, retained traditional American rights intact. Watergate subverted, in secrecy, popular control of government in the United States. Harold Lasswell's prophetic essay of 1941, "The Garrison State," should be reread with care. It is reprinted in Michael P. Smith, ed., *American Politics and Public Policy* (1973).

White House Involvement in Watergate: The burglary of Ellsberg's psychiatrist's office, tardily disclosed, spoiled the evidence against Ellsberg, and the prosecution was dismissed.

Segretti's expenses were later found to be defrayed by payments from Richard Nixon's personal attorney, Herbert W. Kalmbach. Early in July 1973, less than a year after the Nixon coronation at the Miami convention, opinion analysts reported that some 70 percent of persons polled believed the President to be implicated personally in the Watergate burglary or the attempted cover-up.

On July 16, 1973, the former Cabinet Secretary, Alexander Butterfield, disclosed that all conversations held by the President at his offices in the White House and in the Executive Office Building since mid 1971 had been electronically taped. All conversations on the President's business telephones were also recorded. Those who conversed with the President were not told of the recordings, and too late, on July 20, the taping devices were ordered removed. President Nixon refused to surrender tapes to the Ervin Committee and successfully avoided compliance with the committee subpoena. The White House also refused to provide certain tapes to the special prosecutor, but after losing a decision in the District of Columbia Court of Appeals, the President chose not to pursue an appeal to the Supreme Court. Thus a constitutional crisis was averted by accepting the verdict that the President is not above the law. The tapes are being turned over.

By December 1973 only one member of Nixon's original cabinet remained, and that member, George Schultz, moved from Labor to Treasury. Nixon has appointed more members to his cabinet than any other President, thirty-one in five years.

Conclusions

The contemporary American presidency arose, as previously discussed, in direct response to the national unification which swept America as a result of its participation in World War II. Because the traditional presidency emphasized *ad hoc* solutions to problems or crises, the old institution of prewar years was unsuited to the newly nationalized tasks which confronted the postwar Chief Executive. The traditional presidency, as it existed until Truman's incumbency, addressed itself solely to conserving and preserving those values commonly supposed to be a permanent fixture of American life: the American enterprise system of modified capitalism and the quasi-popular control of government through limited enfranchisement of voters.

The contemporary presidency differs from the traditional presidency in its willingness to substitute policy for the previously temporary, intermittent, or transitory exercise of various presidential powers. The chief characteristic of the contemporary institution lies in its studied choice of national goals and public announcement of the means to attain the stated objectives. Inherent in substituting policy for intermittent presidential activity is the willingness to centralize the direction of American life. Harry S Truman's homely motto, "The buck stops here!" is a succinct distillation of the political and administrative philosophy which distinguishes the contemporary presidency. In those simple words Truman announced his intent to create a unified national policy and to accept responsibility for the consequences.

HARRY S TRUMAN

The years 1948 and 1949 mark the watershed of the American presidency. Up to 1949 it is proper to speak of the presidential powers as they were wielded in response to real or imagined situations; by the end of 1949 the choices open to the President had been fused into national policy, which required for its success a unified and permanent presidential authority. Truman's centralization of his authority under the Reorganization Act of 1949, the Employment Act of 1946, and the National Security Act of 1947, coupled with America's predominance in world affairs, placed the President of the United States at the pinnacle of authority and responsibility. In 1949, under the leadership of Harry S Truman, America entered the era of presidential government in the United States. Truman's immediate predecessors were of a different mold. Herbert Hoover had presided unsuccessfully and unhappily over a nation torn by economic failure, sectional disunity, and a lost sense of purpose. Franklin Roosevelt had conducted his office with imaginative leadership, better success, and with magnificent courage and self-confidence; but he was a transitional figure still anxious to conserve and preserve the old values.

The national agenda, announced as policy by Truman in 1945 and again in 1948 and 1949, was a modernized version of the earlier frontier radicalism of the Middle Border, formed during the two decades before 1900 in the crucible of unbounded optimism, unforeseen extremities of weather and rain, and the rapaciousness of corporations and vested interests. Like its populist forebearers, the Fair Deal had no fear of government; it was regarded as a neutral instrument to be intelligently directed and efficiently employed. Because the Fair Deal prized the individual citizen above property rights, the major task of government, indeed its ultimate task, was to redistribute wealth in the nation, and thus to create equality of political, social, and economic opportunity. Modern populism diverges from the old populism in its willingness to move forward to a new time of social, political, and economic opportunity amidst the plenty of the world's most productive industrial and agricultural nation. The Fair Deal put away earlier populist visions of the "agrarian myth," in which honest tillers of the soil lived in a golden age; rather, the Fair Deal combined idealistic goals with realistic analyses and addressed itself to the problems of distributing the fruits of abundance.

The Fair Deal set forth by Truman was a statement of policy, not an episodic reaction to events. The program accurately reflected Truman's central beliefs about the nation and his reply to the question: Why does America exist? In posing the question and providing a clear response, Truman set the standard by which all Presidents since 1945 must be judged. For Truman, the purpose of the nation was "to make life more worthwhile" for all Americans through full use of federal authority. The Fair Deal demanded equality of opportunity for all Americans, sharing and redistributing the national wealth, and harnessing the American economy to national purposes. Precisely because Truman saw the tasks of the nation in terms of overriding national policy, he is the first contemporary American President.

From colonial days until the present it has been customary for state and federal governments to engage in gigantic give-away programs to railroads, to lumber companies, to ranchers, to mining companies, to farmers, to broadcasters, and to businessmen. By 1948 there was little more of the national property to be distributed, and Truman's call for a redistribution of wealth in the nation was denounced in the Senate by Robert A. Taft as a "radical" proposal. The nation's leading Republican was correct in his terminology, but the Fair Deal was not, as Taft saw it, an attack on private property or economic freedom. The Fair Deal was radical because it insisted that Americans create a new society devoted to improving the lot of all Americans rather than the few. The Fair Deal was radical in the classic sense—it went to the roots of American politics, economics, and society and demanded that inequities and injustices of long standing be remedied. Finally, the Fair Deal was radical in that it placed upon every American both the opportunity and the responsibility to advance the national agenda. The Fair Deal insisted that the forms of democracy are meaningless when they are void of social and economic opportunity.

Truman's clearest statement of the philosophy of the Fair Deal came in a campaign address delivered in Saint Louis on October 31, 1948. The speech is a classic attack upon conservatives, corporations, special interests, and the "kept press." In tone it carries the fervor of the old frontier radicalism, and its words decry the "smear campaign on your President . . . in all its vile and untruthfully slanted headlines, columns, and editorials." The President held up to shame the "Hearst character assassins," the "McCormick-Patterson saboteurs," and the conservative columnists who participated in attacks on Truman, not out of their true beliefs but "because they were paid to do it." Truman spoke of the prosperity of the nation and the attempts by Republicans to destroy the unity of farmers with industrial labor. He even identified for his hearers the cause of the high cost of living: "It's the fellow in between who is getting too much profit."

Truman's explanation of the 1948 campaign would have delighted "Sockless Jerry" Simpson, William Jennings Bryan, and Huey Long: "I have told the people that there is just one big issue in this campaign, and that's the people against the special interests." He charged that the Republican Eightieth Congress had passed a "fake housing bill," a "rich man's tax bill," and had done nothing except what "these good-for-nothing lobbies" had asked them to do. The summary was delivered in Truman's flat Missouri twang:

> *People are waking up that the tide is beginning to roll, and I am here to tell you that if you do your duty as citizens of the greatest Republic the sun has even shone on, you will have a Government that will be for your interests, that will be for peace in the world, and for the welfare of all people, and not just a few.*

Truman interpreted his victory in 1948 as a mandate to pursue the Fair Deal. His State of the Union message of January 1949 called on Congress to enact his program and achieve social justice in America within the decade. Like other Presidents before and since, Truman found that his demands for legislation did not bring forth congressional cooperation. The Eighty-first Congress, numerically dominated by Democrats, contained Dixiecrats excited by talk of "states' rights" and unwilling to cooperate in Truman's use of federal powers. The campaign had been abrasive, and Republicans looked for their chance to even the score with the man who had beaten them almost single-handedly. Two issues—one which had all the elements of high comedy were it not for the tragedy which ensued, the other a forthright exercise of the presidential authority—prevented the enactment of the Fair Deal into law. The first was the "Red scare" of the 1950s, which combined credulity, quackery, and buffoonery on a massive scale with character assassination and guilt by association. The second was our intervention in South Korea, a military campaign begun and continued solely by presidential authority. The composition of the Congress, together with the sensational new issues, conspired to make Truman a failure in obtaining the specific programs of the Fair Deal. Nonetheless, Truman had invented the instrument essential to gaining the national agenda when he created the contemporary American presidency; and his programs would eventually be enacted into law.

DWIGHT D. EISENHOWER

Dwight David Eisenhower came to the presidency convinced that he had been elected to destroy and dismantle both the New Deal and the Fair Deal; he had no desire to move forward the Truman agenda. Instead, he perceived the Truman years as an era of "paternalism" and "creeping socialism" which ought to be ended, but he quickly learned that his Republican majorities in the Congress were possessed of an ingrained refusal to cooperate with a President. They were especially unwilling to accept leadership from a general who persisted in denouncing "politicians" as less than respectable. By early 1954 Eisenhower despaired of giving domestic leadership, and the return of Democrats to control of Congress in 1954 forced Eisenhower to busy himself with foreign policy. From 1955 until he left office in 1961 Eisenhower virtually abdicated domestic initiative to the powerful Texans who led the House and the Senate. By 1961 there had been a cautious but firm advancement of some of the goals of the Fair Deal by Sam Rayburn and Lyndon Johnson, with the formal approval of the President. When Eisenhower left the White House, he could claim some social advances in housing, social security, and highways, even as he engaged in a surprising attack on the "military-industrial complex."

JOHN F. KENNEDY

John F. Kennedy entered the White House motivated by his desire for public service and with full understanding that the presidential authority was the proper instrument of reform. Kennedy was a liberal rather than a radical. He was keenly intelligent, dispassionate in his analysis of problems, and well prepared for the office through reading and study. He consciously excluded emotion from his plans and decisions, although he possessed a well-developed sense of social justice. His program, the New Frontier, took the same direction as the Fair Deal, but it lacked the fury of anger against entrenched privilege which characterized Harry Truman. Kennedy's personality, appearance, youth, and style permitted him to mobilize latent American idealism in support of projects which were ethically correct and socially desirable. He fulfilled, better than any President of this century, the role of philosopher-king for the American people. Not the least of his attributes were his attractive family and his enjoyment of his role as President, but his ability to inspire did not extend to members of Congress. At the time of his assassination his projects languished in congressional committees. Had he lived, he might have obtained congressional majorities sufficient to enact his program, and he might also have been converted to frontier radicalism. But what he might have done is mere conjecture; the tragic fact is that he was murdered before he accomplished his work.

LYNDON B. JOHNSON

Upon the death of John F. Kennedy, the presidential office and authority came to a man of passion and commitment to the radicalism of the frontier, Lyndon B. Johnson. Johnson shared the thinking of Long, Norris, Rayburn, and Truman. He had served in government since his youth, and he saw his authority as the ultimate instrument with which to achieve the frontier values of individual freedom and equality of access to property, education, social standing, and political competence. As Senate Majority Leader under Eisenhower, he successfully conquered the racism which had flawed his early career. As Kennedy's successor, Johnson skillfully guided the New Frontier programs through the Congress and signed them into law, but it was as President in his own right that Johnson made the great gains which almost fulfilled the goals of the Fair Deal. Lyndon Johnson's Great Society, which he pushed through Congress in 1965 and early 1966, succeeded in writing into law every program proposed by Truman except full medical care for every American as a matter of right and law. By 1965, Johnson had risen from the presidency to become virtual proprietor of the nation.

America did not, however, become the utopia envisioned by Truman and Johnson. Many of the programs of the Great Society foundered on the rocks of bureaucratic resistance, obfuscation, or plain incompetence. The expectations of those people formerly excluded from full participation in American life rose rapidly, and fulfillment of them was impossible in such short time. Other Americans saw the gains of formerly submerged citizens as a direct threat to the middle class. Those who found Lyndon Johnson personally unattractive or his programs too radical were provided both an excuse and a weapon with which to attack the President after he chose, early in 1965, to send American forces into combat in South Vietnam. With full support of public opinion but without his knowledge or that of any other competent group of advisers, Johnson blundered into the quagmire of Indochina.

The effect of the escalation of the Indochina War was to poison the national idealism and dedication to public service essential to the success of the Great Society. Magnifying the malignant nature of the war was Lyndon Johnson's attempt to be what he was not. Whether of his own volition or on the advice of others, the President forgot that he had been elected by an overwhelming majority of voters in 1964 who admired the boundless energy and deep passion for social justice exhibited by Lyndon Johnson, frontier radical. In mid 1966 Johnson's new infatuation with consensus became a fixation and caused him to attempt to please everyone on every occasion; he ended by pleasing no one. His desire to appear "statesmanlike" was directly responsible for the credibility gap so mercilessly exploited by the media. His outstanding political skills, devalued by his studied projection of seriousness and honesty, were labeled mere "wheeling and dealing." In the face of dissent and opposition Johnson's self-confidence deserted him; military reverses immobilized his choices at the moment his instincts told him to reassess the Indochina War; his control of Congress deteriorated into a charade as he tried to "rise above politics"; and he became entrapped in the snare of projecting a "presidential image." Johnson left the presidency by his own choice, his greatness unrecognized.

RICHARD M. NIXON

Richard M. Nixon, inaugurated in 1969, pledged to "bring us together." In his long political career Nixon had exhibited no desire to accept, much less achieve, the Truman agenda. Instead, he avoided direct solutions to problems, preferring to transform them by managerial means. Early in his tenure Nixon succumbed to the common presidential desire to reorganize the federal apparatus, and he announced the New American Revolution to end the war, to strengthen the states, to make the Supreme Court less liberal, and to bring new efficiency to the federal bureaucracy. Nixon is unique as the only President ever to twice take the oath of office without even nominal majorities of his own party in Congress. As in the Eisenhower years, the President's lack of congressional majorities has confined his main thrust to foreign affairs. The New American Revolution lies quietly in the committees of Congress with little White House pressure to move it toward enactment. The President has had to resort to negative measures, such as impoundment of funds, refusal to operate programs mandated by Congress, and unwillingness to fully staff various departments and agencies. Such negative activism has not fared well in the courts. The Constitution confers extreme flexibility on the Chief Executive as maker of foreign policy, but it is unthinkable that stable foreign policy can be founded on a shifting domestic base.

Domestically, the Nixon administration has been characterized by the failure of serial "game plans" to achieve their stated goals of ending inflation, reducing unemployment, establishing fiscal integrity, and converting the economy to peace without depression. Nixon remains, however, an extremely pragmatic politician, and he may yet advance the national agenda of social justice if he sees such action as essential to the unification of the nation. His reelection of 1972, based on the peculiar mandate, has been negated by the Watergate conspiracy. The President's credibility, whether he ends up as criminal or dupe, has been fatally affected by the conspiracy and his failure to exert the moral leadership necessary to prevent the plot.

THE FUTURE OF
THE PRESIDENCY

The future of the contemporary American presidency is less obscure in the area of problems than solutions. Future Presidents must obtain a socially acceptable means of providing medical care for the American people while successfully cutting through the bureaucratic pollution which frustrated the programs of the Great Society. Perceived racial threats, the lack of evenhanded justice in the courts, and the general distrust of government at all levels must be eliminated. Inequality of opportunity, social discrimination, and the submergence of the individual in an increasingly corporate society, all provide major challenges to those who will take up the presidential authority and responsibility.

The most promising means of success, as presently seen, lies in operating an open administration which avoids both secrecy and the appearance of secrecy. Obviously it is naïve to expect that all matters of policy can be discussed in open forum with the American people or that the President should become a mere servant of public opinion, which is often mercurial. An open administration, such as that of Harry S Truman, carries with it the risk of polarizing public opinion, but it also provides the benefit of determining the will of the people. Openness of administration also avoids pursuit of the will-o'-the-wisp of consensus, while it tends to build an active coalition of popular support on which workable government depends. The future President must also embark upon a major educational effort to teach the American people to observe the workings of their government and to assess the impact of government on the individual citizen. The educational campaign will run afoul of disheartening setbacks, solemn assurances that it cannot succeed, and a high degree of disinterest on the part of those most ignorant of politics. Yet, if popular control of government is to be a reality rather than a pretense, the voter must be able to make his choices on the basis of knowledge rather than emotion or habit.

In the light of the inconclusive nature of the elections of 1960 and 1968, the question of who shall become President assumes prime importance. It is generally agreed that the nominating system now used by both parties, the high costs of campaigning for the nomination and the presidency, and the low level of voter participation indicate the need for reform. Federal funds should be spent in a major drive to register voters; the selection process by which both parties choose delegates should be brought closer to current thinking by election of delegates in a general poll held within forty-five days of the opening of the national convention; and both parties' registration procedures should be altered to attract the widest possible participation in party affairs. Although the recently enacted limitations on presidential campaign spending are a start toward reform, we should look forward to eventual federal funding of campaigns, coupled with strong constraints on spending, as a sensible solution to the campaign problem.

Preemption of prime television time for candidates, mandatory question sessions at which the candidates meet with unscreened voters and the press, and required debate between and among candidates would do much to aid voter choice. If debate is required by law, the incumbent President should be exempt, in deference to the office he holds. Full disclosure of the financial status of each candidate should be required as well as the reporting of all conflicts of interest. All reforms should have as their object the opening up of opportunities to qualified candidates regardless of their financial resources and the provision of better information to the voters.

The future President will have to move beyond the Truman agenda, as Truman advanced beyond the liberalism of Wilson and Franklin Roosevelt. The Truman proposals, only recently enacted, were announced a generation ago and were suited to those times and conditions. Indeed, the failure to make more rapid progress in achieving Truman's national agenda has exacerbated America's problems, making their solution increasingly more difficult. Worse, Americans have blinded themselves to developments in American life which present a clear danger to the individual as well as the democracy. In this day, American society and the economy suffer a burgeoning corporateness which threatens to overwhelm the individual and destroy his primacy in this nation. During the past two decades the hundred largest corporations have gained control of over half the nation's corporate assets, a greater proportion than was vested in the largest 200 corporations in 1950. Even if we Americans should reform our political process and achieve a universal democracy, we stand to lose all if we permit the rending of the social fabric of the nation and the reduction of the economy to a feudal structure.

This is an era of increasing concentration of wealth and economic power vested in huge corporations and multinational conglomerates which have long since escaped control by their owners, a time in which the national ecology is being destroyed by irresponsible gathering and usage of resources, and a period when large segments of American people are disaffected from the traditional loyalty to the nation by injustices too long uncorrected. We have undergone a noticeable deterioration of the quality of goods and services; our transportation system is unable to provide essential carrying services for people and goods; our price structure has become startlingly inflexible through lessened competition and administered prices; and cries are heard to eliminate foreign competitors, because American industry can no longer compete in the domestic market. The future President will have to give his attention to those developments which have produced this present crisis of authority, trust, and self-confidence.

Ending the war in Indochina, essential to rebuilding national unity, will not solve America's present difficulties nor those of the future. Instead, long-term solutions require us to adopt new policies capable of providing safeguards for the individual, for society, and for the democratic process.

The future President of the United States must intervene in large enterprises which dominate markets, serve as "price leaders" for their industry, have major impact on the rigid price structure of the nation, or pose permanent threats to the ecology. Presidential intervention in organizations, to be defined by law as being "directly affected with a public interest," may take the form of appointing sufficient public members to the board of directors of such enterprises to protect the public interest. Such firms or corporations should be required to observe the principle of "prudent management" and follow prescribed accounting methods in reports to Congress and the President. Most of the present regulatory agencies of the federal government should be eliminated, as they have long since become captives of the industries they were created to regulate.

Our current economic crisis also reflects subtle changes which have occurred in American labor-management relations during the past ten to fifteen years. Lengthy strikes, except in admittedly "sick" industries like transportation services, have not been the rule. A surface appraisal of the apparently "healthy" great industries indicates a beneficial industrial era of peace, but all is not well. There has grown up and there continues to grow a friendly alliance of the managers of large enterprise and the leaders of major unions. In the past decade price leadership in industry has been emulated by the unions, and "wage leadership" has become a way of life. The United Auto Workers offer the best example of wage leadership in their custom of striking a single automobile corporation, gaining a favorable wage settlement, and applying the same "wage package" to other manufacturers, who simply fall in line. This "sweetheart" arrangement has had the effect of eliminating automation or sophisticated fabrication equipment as alternative methods of production, increasing the costs of labor relative to productivity, reducing profits returned to stockholders, and raising the price of almost every product of giant enterprise. The major corporations have no difficulty in maintaining production; union wage packages constantly increase; and high prices in American markets attract foreign competition. Increasingly, from the throats of both management and labor, arise cries for protection from foreign competition. Other industries, particularly electronics and optics, have confessed failure and produce goods abroad to be marketed at home under well-advertised American brand names.

Of equal priority with corporate reform is the long-needed reform of the federal tax structure. Due to the patch-work of special changes and amendments adopted since the 1930s, the present tax system has developed significant methods and means by which the tax burden is shifted from those individuals and corporations best able to pay to those legally unable to avoid tax liabilities. Two results of utmost gravity and concern have already appeared: growing discontent among middle-income taxpayers, who are unduly burdened, and budget-making in terms of revenues available rather than on the basis of needed services. Tax avoidance, at once a science and a lucrative career for lawyers and accountants, carries with it the twin dangers of channeling capital into socially undesirable activities and denying to government the funds essential to carrying out the purposes of the nation.

The present mishmash of taxation also precludes, by its very operation, any significant redistribution of wealth through progressive taxation. Worse, our present federal tax inequities hold over us the ever-present threat of a national sales tax, which is totally regressive. The value-added tax, discussed for years as a painless method of extracting huge revenues from the taxpayers, places the entire burden upon the consumer, while the hypothecators, moneylenders, and securities operators remain exempt. The poor may yet spend their way to riches, but not in the foreseeable future.

In view of the history of transportation in the United States, we have already passed the point at which we can afford the luxury of private ownership of the various modes. The society has become so interdependent and the economy so complex that we need to rationalize services, provide true intermodal competition, and develop a schedule of pricing which accurately reflects the cost of the service rendered. Private ownership of some firms has become a travesty due to subsidies, while others, particularly those engaged in mass transit, are a tragedy. Like interstate highways or national defense, the transportation problem is simply too large and complex for private management. Government purchase of transportation properties and their equipment, at actual cash value, is the first step in achieving transportation adequate to the national needs.

The future President will need to reorganize the present governmental structure. Reorganization has long been the universally prescribed remedy for the nation's ills, but were this true, we would long since have achieved utopia. The present federal structure is bloated in size, sometimes redundant in function, and often inefficient in spite of the best efforts of dedicated employees. A careful and detailed analysis of the scope and function of each federal activity and agency, with a sensible study of the types and numbers of personnel needed, can provide valid guides to reorganization. What is to be avoided is a battle cry like, "Decentralization now!"; or the magic number approach, "Reduce spending by 8.214963 percent"; or, "Where's the meat-ax, Joe?" Greater efficiency, including unremitting control of pricing and supply practices of purveyors of goods and services to government, should be the object of reorganization.

The future President must achieve more complete fiscal control of government, particularly because the continuing nationalization of American life will bring an attendant increase in federal tasks. The most fruitful approach lies in the separation of budget-making for recurrent expenses from that for proposed new budgetary items or nonrecurring expenditures. The fixed expenses of the federal establishment can be calculated with accuracy from year to year, scaled upward or downward to reflect changes in prices or interest, and passed without debate by Congress. By this means, Congress could free itself to investigate new proposals, nonrecurring projects, or significant changes in existing programs at the same time it avoids the pressures of the present unitary budget. An important benefit of separate budgeting would be reform of present congressional authorization and appropriation practices and greater congressional oversight of actual budgetary change. In the interest of obtaining a single money manager for the nation, the powers of the Board of Governors of the Federal Reserve System should be transferred to the Executive Office of the President.

The future President would do well to invite the involvement of all Americans, except those obviously unfit, in their government. He should propose a national participation law, to operate without discrimination, which would require that every American spend two years in federal service at some time between his eighteenth and thirty-fifth birthdays. Each person reporting for service would be classified and directed into an area of government in which his talents could best be employed. All persons serving in any given year would be paid the same nominal salary regardless of qualifications, except that a premium wage would be paid to those engaged in actual combat duty in time of war.

Many unskilled citizens would choose to enter service at age eighteen, and receive exposure to successful people in government and firsthand observation of career possibilities while gaining valuable experience. Others might choose to complete college, graduate school, or professional training before electing to serve, enabling the government to obtain their services at nominal cost. The advantage to government of such obligated service would lie in its constant exposure to new ideas and in challenges to time-honored methods. The individual would benefit by having been personally involved in his government, and he could come away with a sense of having repaid the nation for the unparalleled advantages of being an American citizen.

The policy alternatives discussed above are not meant as an all-inclusive listing of the tasks which will confront future Presidents. On the contrary, they represent only those national problems which have already emerged and which call for national action at this time. Other areas beyond Truman's national agenda will undoubtedly assert themselves, but any President who operates an open administration, takes care to counsel with the people, and possesses the intelligence and will to administer his authority on a rational basis can be a success for himself and his nation. One who can bring to the task wit, graciousness, compassion, and understanding can achieve greatness.

NOTES

Populism: The best short treatment of populism's origins and development, as well as a sympathetic assessment of W. J. Bryan, is in Paul W. Glad, *McKinley, Bryan, and the People* (1964).

Truman's St. Louis Speech: Truman's speech at Kiel Auditorium, his last major address of the 1948 campaign, is reprinted in J. A. Garraty and R. A. Divine, *Twentieth-Century America* (1968), pp. 520–526.

Eisenhower's Memoirs: The Eisenhower memoir of the White House years was entitled, significantly, *Mandate for Change* (1963).

The Kennedy Era: No satisfying study of John F. Kennedy has yet been made, although Arthur Schlesinger, Jr., in *A Thousand Days* (1965), has provided a compendium of Kennedy's era.

Lyndon Johnson's Incumbency: Eric Goldman's *Tragedy of Lyndon Johnson* (1968) is a facile study which raises serious questions regarding its seemingly contrived thesis.

Studies of Nixon: Most studies of Richard M. Nixon suffer from prejudice, hatred, or the desire to denigrate Nixon as politician and man. A truly unbiased analysis of Nixon has not yet been written.

Need for Administration Openness: Distrust of government at all levels is documented in the Harris poll commissioned by Senator Edmund Muskie's Intergovernmental Relations subcommittee. The poll, completed in the summer of 1973, concludes that the American people are certain of the value of the present system of government and that they know how its present ills may be remedied. Those sampled want integrity of leaders, open access to broad popular participation in government at all levels, and an end to secrecy which can exclude citizen participation and subvert individual freedom. What is wanted is "a strong federal government to get this country moving again," but with added reliance on state and local governments.

The Effects of Elections: A fresh view of the effect of particular elections, based on quantitative analysis, is W. D. Burnham's *Critical Elections* (1970). Burnham propounds his theory of critical realignments in American politics.

Voter Behavior: Fred I. Greenstein's *The American Party System and the American People* (second edition, 1970), presents a succinct and cogent short treatment of voter behavior in recent elections.

Corporate Control: The most scholarly recent work on the great corporations and industries, Joe S. Bain, *Industrial Organization* (1959), regards industrial concentration after 1935 as in a condition of stability. See pp. 201–209.

Labor Control: Part of the deterioration of American industry must be traced, although no study is available, to the "sweetheart" nature of labor contracts in America's great industries and the neo-Luddite fear of automation among American union leaders.

Tax Reforms: Reforms on capital gains and absolute taxes on incomes over $200,000 annually, which took effect in 1972, threaten certain tax shelters, but the reform is minimal in effect.

Power in Business and Government: See Grant McConnell's careful analysis of the quest for power and its use in business and industry in his *Private Power and American Democracy* (1966), Chapter 8. Harold Seidman, in his *Politics, Position, and Power* (1970), offers a knowledgeable inside view of the intricacies of power considerations within the federal bureaucracy.

Federal Fiscal Reform: An exhaustive and perceptive advocacy of budgetary and fiscal reform in the federal structure is contained in A. B. Wildavsky, *The Politics of the Budgetary Process* (1964).

INDEX